JOACHIM PEIPER AND THE NAZI ATROCITIES OF 1944

JOACHIM PEIPER AND THE NAZI ATROCITIES OF 1944

STEPHEN WYNN

Pen & Sword
MILITARY
AN IMPRINT OF PEN & SWORD BOOKS LTD.
YORKSHIRE – PHILADELPHIA

First published in Great Britain in 2022 by
Pen & Sword Military
An imprint of
Pen & Sword Books Limited
Yorkshire - Philadelphia

ISBN 978 1 52673 7 113

A CIP catalogue record for this book is available from the British Library

Typeset in Ehrhardt MT 11.5/14 by
Sjmagic DESIGN SERVICES, India.

Printed and bound in the UK by
CPI Group (UK) Ltd, Croydon, CR0 4YY

Pen & Sword Books Limited incorporates the imprints of Atlas,
Archaeology, Aviation, Discovery, Family History, Fiction, History, Maritime,
Military, Military Classics, Politics, Select, Transport, True Crime, Air World,
Frontline Publishing, Leo Cooper, Remember When, Seaforth Publishing,
The Praetorian Press, Wharncliffe Local History, Wharncliffe Transport,
Wharncliffe True Crime and White Owl.

For a complete list of Pen & Sword titles please contact
PEN & SWORD BOOKS LIMITED
47 Church Street, Barnsley, South Yorkshire S70 2AS, United Kingdom
E-mail: enquiries@pen-and-sword.co.uk
Website: www.pen-and-sword.co.uk

Or

PEN AND SWORD BOOKS
1950 Lawrence Rd, Havertown, PA 19083, USA
E-mail: Uspen-and-sword@casematepublishers.com
Website: www.penandswordbooks.com

Contents

Introduction

With the rise of Adolf Hitler and the Nazi Party in 1933, there were many who readily signed up to become members of the Party; men and women who had previously been intelligent, hard-working, upstanding members of German society.

One such man was Heinrich Luitpold Himmler, one of the main proponents of the Holocaust, who went on to become not only a leading member of the Nazi Party as the Reichsführer of the Schutzstaffel, better known as the SS, but one of the most powerful individuals in Nazi Germany.

Heinrich Himmler was the middle of three sons born to Joseph and Anna Himmler on 7 October 1900 in Munich, Germany. They were what would have been classed as a conservative, middle-class family in German society, where Joseph worked as a teacher and Anna brought their three sons up as part of a Godfearing, devout Roman Catholic family.

Himmler and his two brothers, Gebhard and Ernst, all attended the local grammar school in Landshut, Bavaria, where their father was the deputy principal. He was remembered as a studious boy, but one who had a history of bad health, which possibly explained his feeling of awkwardness in social situations.

According to Peter Longerich in *Heinrich Himmler: A Life*, Himmler's diaries showed he was interested in matters such as current affairs, the debate that surrounded the somewhat delicate connection between religion and sex, and the chivalrous sport of duelling.

Just two months past his seventeenth birthday, he enlisted in the reserve battalion of the 11th Bavarian Regiment, as an 'officer candidate'. When Germany finally capitulated and surrendered on 11 November 1918, Himmler was still undergoing his basic military training, so he did not get to see active service and was discharged from the army a month later.

He had not yet shown any sign of the man he would become. In 1919 he became a student at what is today the Technical University of Munich, where he studied agronomy, the science and technology of producing and using plants in agriculture for food, fuel, fibre and land restoration.

By the time he became a student, Himmler already held anti-Semitic views after reading a polemic by Friedrich Wichtl which blamed Freemasons for the outcome of the First World War and cited strong Jewish influence in freemasonry. In his diary he notes that it was a book which 'sheds light on everything and tells who we have to fight first'. Despite this, he still managed to maintain a politeness towards fellow students who were of the Jewish faith. There was no sign yet of the infamous Himmler the world would come to know.

It would appear that the change and hardening of Himmler's views in relation to the 'Jewish question' can be traced back to 1922. Although he had wanted to become a doctor, he ended up with a diploma in agriculture. It was during his continued educational studies that politically Himmler began veering towards the radical right. He joined the Nazi Party in 1923, and in 1925 he became a member of the SS.

This is a potted history of Himmler's early years, and he is mentioned only to provide an example of how it was possible for a child born into a conservative, Christian, well respected family and who obtained a diploma in agriculture, went on to become the architect of the murder of an estimated 6 million Jews in the Holocaust. The reason I have used Himmler's story specifically as an example of the journey from normality to borderline madness taken by a number of Germans, is because Joachim Peiper was Himmler's adjutant during the Second World War.

But Himmler was just one of hundreds, if not thousands of German men who followed a similar path from obscurity to infamy. In the years immediately following the end of the war, there were a number of trials of Germans who, it was alleged, had committed war crimes against either European civilians or Allied military personnel, while serving in the ranks of the Third Reich.

This book will consider Peiper's career in the SS, his time spent as Himmler's adjutant, his time in the SS Division Leibstandarte and his involvement in the Battle of Normandy; the Battle of the Bulge; the Boves massacre in Italy in September 1943; and the massacres in Malmedy, Honsfeld, Bullingen, Ligneuville, Stavelot, Cheneux, La Gleize, Wereth and Stoumont, which took place between 17 and 20 December 1944. It will also consider his arrest, interrogation, trial, imprisonment, and later life after his eventual release from incarceration.

Chapter One

Leibstandarte SS Adolf Hitler (LSSAH)

In early 1923, Adolf Hitler decided that he needed an elite bodyguard of men for his personal protection. Originally it consisted of just eight men and came under the command of one Julius Schreck, who had been a member of the Nazi Party since its formation, and became a close friend, confidant and devotee of Adolf Hitler, to such an extent that he even had the same style of moustache – no wider than the width of his nostrils.

On 4 April 1925, Schreck became the first leader of the newly formed Schutzstaffel or 'Protection Squadron; SS'. Prior to this the organisation had names such as Sturmabteilung, 'Storm Detachment; SA'; Stabswache, 'Staff Guard'; Stosstrupp-Hitler, 'Shock Troop-Hitler'; Schutzkommando, 'Protection Command'; and Sturmstaffel, 'Storm Squadron'.

To be readily distinguishable from other units the Schutzstaffel took to wearing Armanen runes, in the form of two italic 'S's' on the collars of their uniforms, as well as a skull insignia as its cap badge.

Besides the General SS, who were tasked with enforcing the racial policies of Nazi Germany, and the Waffen-SS, which were fighting units, there was also the Totenkopfverbände, or the 'Death Head' units, which were responsible for Nazi Germany's concentration and extermination camps, which oversaw the murder of an estimated 6 million victims, most of whom were Jewish.

The German military system does appear to have been somewhat complicated. The Wehrmacht, which had replaced the pre-Nazi era Reichswehr, already had its military elements in the form of the Heer, Kriegsmarine and Luftwaffe, or army, navy and air force, so why it needed the Waffen-SS as a second German army is unclear.

To be considered as an officer in the SS, candidates had to be able to provide proof of their Aryan ancestry back to 1750, and for men in the rank and file, the same was required back to 1800, although once the war began, this was changed to candidates having to prove the same back only to their grandparents.

Jumping forward for a second to the Malmedy massacre during the Ardennes Offensive in December 1944, and mention of the 'Hitler Order' to act with aggression and terror, it is maybe worth pointing out here that it had always been part of the SS ideology to use brutality and terror rather than military and political methods. In fact the SS were actually entrusted with carrying out atrocities and illegal activities which amounted to war crimes.

Between 30 June and 2 July 1934, as part of Operation Hummingbird, better known as the 'Night of the Long Knives', the LSSAH, under the direct day-to-day command of Sepp Dietrich, were used to carry out a number of extrajudicial political executions, which had been ordered by Adolf Hitler. These killings were carried out as a direct result of Stabchef-SA Ernst Rohm (the man in charge of the Sturmabteilung (SA)) pushing to have greater political influence, something which did not sit well with Adolf Hitler who, along with Hermann Goering and Heinrich Himmler, saw this as a direct challenge to the power of the Nazi Party and of Hitler himself.

Hitler arranged a fictitious meeting at the Hanselbauer Hotel in the small Spa town of Bad Wiessee in Bavaria, and ordered that senior SA leaders should attend. At the meeting, Ernst Rohm, Anton von Hohberg und Buchwald, Kalr Ernst, Edmund Heines, and Peter von Heydebreck were all arrested and taken to Stadelheim Prison in Munich. Later that same day, all of those who had been arrested at the Hanselbauer Hotel, except Rohm, were executed by a firing squad made up of a number of LSSAH men, in the courtyard at Stadelheim prison. Ernst Rohm was executed the following day.

By the end of the three-day purge, a number of Hitler's opponents and critics had been murdered by elements of the LSSAH under Himmler, the Gestapo under Reinhard Heydrich, and Goering's personal police battalion. Estimations on the number of people who had been killed varied wildly, from 85 to as many as 1,000. To commemorate their actions as part of the Night of the Long Knives, the LSSAH were increased in size to that of a regiment.

The LSSAH were also involved in:

1935 Reoccupation of the Saarland.
1938 Marched in to Austria.
1938 Reoccupation of the Sudetenland.
1939 Increased in size to a full infantry regiment – three infantry battalions, an artillery battalion, an anti-tank unit, a reconnaissance unit, and an engineer unit.
1939 Occupation of Bohemia and Moldova.
1939 Invasion of Poland.

Before Germany's invasion of Poland, which sparked the beginning of the Second World War, the LSSAH was already an extremely experienced and hardened body of men, dedicated to Adolf Hitler and the Nazi Party and its ideology.

Right from the outbreak of the war, following Germany's invasion of Poland in September 1939, the SS units drew the wrong type of attention. Rather than fighting with their army counterparts, they fought as independent infantry units who seemed more intent on murdering Jewish civilians and setting fire to a number of Polish towns and villages than fighting against the Polish Army. They were responsible for the murder of hundreds of Polish civilians; in the town of Zloczew, along with elements of the 17th Wehrmacht Infantry Division, they killed some 200 men, women and children, for no particular reason other than they could. The dead included both Jews and Christians alike. They also burned and destroyed nearly 250 government buildings, businesses and private homes.

Despite it being known that units of the 17th Wehrmacht Infantry Division and the Leibstandarte SS Adolf Hitler were in Zloczew at the time of the murders, nobody was ever prosecuted because it was claimed that it had not been possible to identify the exact units that had been in the town at the time.

It is quite clear from the outset of the war that the LSSAH conducted itself in a particular manner, clearly showing that such behaviour and conduct was synonymous with a particular unit rather than the specific individuals in charge of it, or members of it. To serve in the unit, a man had to be a member of the Nazi Party and be willing and able to carry out all aspects of the Party's policies. In essence, those who served in the SS were Party fanatics, who were happy to conduct themselves outside of the normal rules of civility, even during a time of war.

The invasion of France saw the LSSAH cross the Dutch border on 10 May 1940, tasked with capturing an important bridge that crossed the River Ijssel, and to link up with German airborne forces. By the time they left Holland on 15 May, they had captured 3,500 Dutch troops.

With the evacuation of the British Expeditionary Force at Dunkirk in full swing, just ten miles away the northern French village of Wormhout was captured by the 2nd Battalion, 1st SS Division, LSSAH, under the command of SS-Hauptsturmführer Wilhelm Mohnke.

With the taking of the village came the surrender of British troops from the 2nd Battalion, Royal Warwickshire, 4th Battalion, Cheshire Regiment, gunners from the 210th Battery, 53rd (The Worcestershire Yeomanry) Anti-Tank Regiment, Royal Artillery who had literally run out of ammunition, along with a number of French troops who had been in charge of a military depot. All of these prisoners of war were taken to a barn in nearby La Plaine au Bois; on the way there, the conduct of the SS troops changed dramatically and they shot a number of wounded British soldiers.

When they reached the barn the prisoners were herded in and the doors were locked behind them. The SS troops then threw in a number of stick grenades and the subsequent explosions killed a number of prisoners; due to the bravery of Sergeant Stanley Moore and Company Sergeant Major Augustus Jennings, who threw their bodies on to some of the grenades, a number of the prisoners were saved.

When the SS troops realised what had happened they called out some of the prisoners and immediately shot them. By the time the incident was over, eighty of the prisoners had been murdered; a further fifteen had been wounded, but within two days, nine of them had died of their wounds. Those who managed to survive were discovered a couple of days later by German army medics, taken to hospital, and spent the rest of the war as prisoners of war.

Nobody from the 2nd Battalion, 1st SS Division, LSSAH, was ever prosecuted in relation to the Wormhout massacre.

In late 1940, the LSSAH underwent amphibious assault training in preparation for the invasion of England: Operation Sea Lion.

In February 1941, the LSSAH were sent to Bulgaria, and later the same year they arrived in Yugoslavia.

The rest of their major involvements in the Second World War are covered in differing degrees elsewhere in this book.

During the six years between 1940 and the end of the war, it is estimated that members of the LSSAH were involved in a number of wartime atrocities, which resulted in the deaths of an estimated 5,000 prisoners of war and civilians.

Chapter Two

Joachim Peiper – Early life

Joachim Peiper was born on 30 January 1915 in Berlin, Germany, where he grew up in a middle-class, Christian family. His father, Waldemar Peiper, had been a military man who served as a captain in the German Imperial Army, and saw action in the colonial campaigns in German East Africa between 1904 and 1908. The troubles had begun when the Nama people, having had enough of being ruled by Germany, rebelled and slaughtered somewhere in the region of one hundred German men in the Okahandja area of what is Namibia today.

Despite his rank, Captain Peiper was often seen fighting alongside his men, which resulted in him being wounded several times and also catching malaria.

When the First World War broke out, Waldemar was once again in military service and was sent out to serve in Turkey; for him it was to be a short war, which came to an abrupt end in 1915 due to poor health, directly related to the bout of malaria he had contracted in East Africa

Waldemar was a brave and a patriotic German who, despite his ailments, joined the Freikorps, or 'Free regiments', when the war ended. The Freikorps were a paramilitary organisation made up of volunteers, first formed in the 1700s, whose members were better described as mercenaries, and who fought and served in any German-speaking nation where armed conflicts broke out.

The immediate aftermath of the First World War saw the beginning of the German Revolution. The Freikorps, which consisted mainly of German veterans, fought on behalf of the Weimar Republic, the German government formed at the end of the war, against German communists who were backed by the Soviet Union in an attempt to overthrow the government.

Waldemar and his comrades fought in the Silesian Uprisings between August 1919 and July 1921. At the time, the area known as Upper Silesia was part of the Weimar Republic, but Polish separatists, who had other ideas, wanted it to become part of the newly formed Polish Republic. After nearly two years of fighting, the result was a stalemate, which resulted in Germany and Poland agreeing to divide the area of Upper Silesia between each other.

The obvious question to ask is why, after the end of the First World War, which resulted in deaths of millions of their peoples, would German and Polish forces be so willing to fight each other? The answer is possibly connected to the wealth and riches which emanated from the region of Upper Silesia, in the form of large mineral deposits. The area was awash with mines which provided Germany with large quantities of commodities such as coal, zinc and lead. Upper Silesia was so important to Germany that when the Treaty of Versailles was being drawn up at the end of the First World War, Germany informed the Allied nations that she would not be able to fulfil her financial obligations to them under the terms of the treaty, without the region of Upper Silesia being officially recognised as being part of Germany.

Waldemar's involvement with the Freikorps coincided with the formation of the National Socialist German Workers Party (NSDAP), better known as the Nazi Party, of which he became a dedicated member. In keeping with Nazi ideology, he was also openly anti-Semitic.

With Waldemar as his father and role model, it could be easily argued that it is little wonder that Joachim Peiper turned out to be what he eventually became.

Joachim's eldest brother Hans, born in 1910, had been a troubled soul for many years and had tried to take his own life while still at high school. Although the attempt failed it left him in a persistent vegetative state, and when he was 21 years of age his parents placed him in a 'mental institution', where he died eleven years later in 1942.

Joachim Peiper was a student of average intelligence who was both diligent and hard-working in an academic sense, but despite his best efforts, his exam results were not quite good enough to gain him a place at university.

While still at school, and along with his other brother Horst, he decided to join the Scouting movement, which was an extremely popular pastime in pre-war Germany. It had begun in 1909, with its numbers rising dramatically after the end of the First World War, continuing to do so until about 1936, when all such organizations were forced to close by the Nazi Party. All members of the Scouting movement had to become members of the Hitler Youth, which Joachim Peiper had already chosen to do in 1933. Not surprisingly, it was in such an environment that Peiper developed his interest in having a military career.

Later the same year on 12 October, by which time he was just three months shy of his nineteenth birthday, Peiper enlisted in the 7th SS Reiterstandarte, or Cavalry Regiment. He did so on the advice of family friend and fervent Nazi, General (later to be Field Marshal) Walter von Reichenau. This, I believe, is an extremely interesting connection to the historical discussion which surrounds Joachim Peiper, and his willingness to engage in the murder of unarmed American prisoners of war, with an apparent lack of empathy and a coldness which allowed no place for regret or self-recrimination.

Walther von Reichenau had enlisted in the German Imperial Army in 1903, and it is more than likely he had served with Peiper's father in German East Africa, which could possibly explain where the 'family friend' connection originated. He had also served during the First World War, seeing action on the Western Front in France, during which time he was awarded the Iron Cross First Class. By the war's end he had been promoted to the rank of captain.

The Treaty of Versailles allowed Germany to maintain an army, or Reichwehr, of no more than 96,000 men. Von Reichenau was one of the 4,000 officers that were included in this number. The treaty did not, however, allow for the post-war German Army to have a General Staff, so they formed the cover organisation, Truppenamt, or 'Troop Office', under the leadership of Major General Hans von Seeckt, who had been the last Chief of the General Staff of the German Imperial Army at the end of the First World War. Reichenau's position within the organisation was that of Chief of Staff to the Inspector of Signals at the Reichwehr Ministry. The Truppenamt remained in place until 1935.

Reichenau was first introduced to Adolf Hitler by an uncle in 1932, and soon after this he joined the Nazi Party, which was forbidden under Army Regulations as set out by Seeckt in order to keep the army out of any involvement in politics, directly or indirectly. There was a certain irony attached to this as Seeckt's own political views could easily be described as far-right, and he chose to ignore Germany's Constitution of 1919 prohibiting the practice of religious discrimination, by ordering that Jews were not allowed to join the Reichswehr.

Reichenau's family owned a factory, which manufactured furniture, on the outskirts of the city of Karlsruhe in north-west Germany. In 1938 they gave the factory to the Nazi Party and its use was changed to that of the manufacture of munitions.

When Adolf Hitler and the Nazi Party came into power in January 1933, Reichenau became head of the Ministerial Office, with his main role being to liaise between the Nazi Party and the German Army. He also became heavily involved in the downfall of Ernst Rohm, who held control over Hitler's 'Brown Shirts' or SA, realising that if the Nazi Party and the German Army were going to have a productive 'marriage', then Rohm had to go, even though he had been a close friend of Hitler's as far back as 1919 when they had both been members of the National Socialist German Workers Party.

In January 1931, at Hitler's personal request, Rohm took charge of the Sturmabteilung (SA), becoming its Chief of Staff and in charge of more than one million men. By giving Rohm this position Hitler also inadvertently signed his death warrant. Rohm became too powerful, and therefore a threat to Hitler's overall power as Führer and, for Hitler to be taken seriously in a political sense, the SA's thuggery and violence could no longer be allowed to openly continue. Rohm openly made statements that would have undoubtedly come to Hitler's attention. In June 1933 Rohm said the following about Hitler:

> Adolf is rotten. He's betraying all of us. He only goes round with reactionaries. His old comrades aren't good enough for him. So he brings in these East Prussian generals. They're the ones he pals around with now. Adolf knows perfectly well what I want. Are we a revolution or aren't we? Something new has to be brought in, understand? The generals are old fogies. They'll never have a new idea.

There was the additional aspect of Rohm being openly homosexual in a time when such matters only went on behind closed doors, and because of the close relationship he'd had with Hitler, rumours began about Hitler's own sexuality. Rohm had to go. He was arrested during the Night of the Long Knives, 29/30 June 1934, and held at Stadelheim prison in Munich where, on 1 July, he was shot dead in his cell by SS-Brigadeführer Theodor Eicke and SS-Obersturmbannführer Michael Lippert.

With the outbreak of the Second World War, Reichenau was given command of the German 10th Army for the invasion of Poland, and by the time of Germany's invasion of Belgium and France, he was in command of the 6th Army.

Even though he did not agree with Germany's invasion of the Soviet Union in June 1941, as head of the 6th Army, he led his men in Operation Barbarossa. The contradiction with his opposition to the invasion going ahead was his support of the Einsatzgruppen and their murdering of Jews as the Germans fought their way across Soviet territory.

If there was any doubt about Richenau's support of Hitler and the madness of his political policies, especially where the Jews were concerned, he made matters abundantly clear when, on 10 October 1941, he issued what became known as the 'Reichenau Order'. Included within it was the following.

> Far from all political considerations of the future, the soldier has two things to fulfil:
> (1) The total annihilation of the Bolshevik madness, the Soviet state and its leaders.
> (2) The merciless extermination of foreign insidiousness and cruelty and thus the safeguarding of the life of the German Wehrmacht in Russia.

> Only in this way will we fulfil our historical task of freeing the German people from the Asian-Jewish danger once and for all.

Six months into Operation Barbarossa an event took place which may well have determined its eventual outcome. On 19 December 1941, and with matters in the Soviet Union not going to plan, Hitler's Commander-in-Chief, Walther von Brauchitsch, suffered a massive heart attack and Hitler was forced to replace him. Even if he hadn't had a heart attack, it is more than likely von Brauchitsch would not have remained as the army's Commander-in-Chief due to his troops inability to capture Moscow.

Following Reichenau's successes in Poland with the 10th Army, and in Belgium and France with the 6th Army, he was Hitler's first choice to replace von Brauchitsch, but senior officers of the German Army were not in favour of such a replacement, and made their collective opinion very clear. Unfortunately for the senior army officers in question, it became a case of 'be careful of what you wish for'; Hitler's second choice for the position was himself, and the outcome of that decision was the beginning of the end for Nazi Germany.

While still in the Soviet Union in January 1942, von Reichenau suffered a cerebral haemorrhage and the decision was taken to have him flown to a hospital in Leipzig, Germany, for further treatment. This is where the circumstances of his death differ depending on which version you choose to believe. There is one story that suggests the aircraft he was being flown in crashed while still over Russian territory; another suggests that during the flight he had a heart attack and died and that the pilot of the aircraft simply carried out an emergency landing. Either way, he was buried in the Invalidenfriedhof Cemetery in Berlin.

For a role model, Joachim Peiper had his father, an anti-Semite who was also an ardent Nazi. In Walther von Reichenau, someone he also looked up to and happily took advice from, he had not only an anti-Semite, but an individual who was more than happy to kill and murder individuals who he perceived posed a threat to Nazi Germany. With this in mind, it is quite conceivable that Peiper would have viewed his own actions in ordering the cold blooded murders of unarmed prisoners of war and members of civilian populations as both normal and acceptable.

On 23 January 1934, just one week before his nineteenth birthday, Joachim Peiper enlisted in the Schutzstaffel at the rank of Mann, which was the lowest possible rank a man could be given when he joined up. He was issued with the service number of 132.496.

The Nuremberg Rally

What is often referred to as the Nuremberg Rally, or the Reich Party Convention, took place at the Luitpoldarena, the Nazi Party's rally grounds located in the south east of Nuremberg, and covered an area some 11 square kilometres in size.

From 1927 onwards all of these rallies were held exclusively at Nuremberg. Prior to this they had been held in Munich between 1923 and 1925, and Weimar in 1926.

Each of the rallies was given a name in keeping with significant national events that had taken place throughout that particular year. The rally of 5–10 September 1934 was not given a name, however, so in subsequent years, rallies were referred to by a variety of different titles including, the 'Rally of Unity and Strength', the 'Rally of Power', or the 'Rally of Will'.

The 1934 rally was the sixth such event and was attended by some 700,000 supporters of the Nazi Party. It was notable for two reasons: first, there was what was known as Albert Speer's 'Cathedral of Light', achieved by the use of 152 giant searchlights which gave the same effect as the walls of a building, and second because a propaganda film was made of that year's event. Released in 1935, it was entitled *Triumph of the Wills*, and was directed by Helene Bertha Amalie 'Leni' Riefenstahl. In 1938 another of her films, *Olympia*, a two-part documentary of the 1936 Summer Olympics, held in the Olympic Stadium in Berlin, was released, bringing her worldwide acclaim as a director.

It was during the 1934 Nuremberg Rally that Peiper was promoted to the rank of SS-Sturmann, and at the same time, came to the attention of the Reichsführer of the Schutzstaffel, Heinrich Himmler, one of the most powerful and influential men throughout Nazi Germany. Despite the fact that Peiper, not the biggest of men in a physical sense, and with black hair, was as far away as was possible from the stereotypical image of a tall, muscular, blond-haired, blue-eyed Aryan, Himmler was certainly taken with him, as what he saw a true German Aryan should be.

In early 1935, Peiper attended a leadership course of the LSSAH, which was Hitler's personal bodyguard. Although he sufficiently impressed his instructors to pass the course, doctors noted in their psychological evaluation of him how he had tried impressing them with his connection to Himmler, and that he was egotistical and prone to adopting a negative attitude in matters that did not interest him. One of their conclusions of Peiper was that he could prove to be an 'arrogant superior'.

One way or another, Peiper was deemed as having the required attributes to become a future SS leader, and between 24 April 1935 and 30 March 1936, he attended a course at the SS Officer Training Camp in the city of Brunswick in Lower Saxony, run by Paul Hausser, who went on to command the 2nd SS Panzer Corps, and became a recipient of the Knights Cross of the Iron Cross with Oak Leaves and Swords

The relevance of this particular course in relation to Peiper and some of his conduct during the Second World War wasn't so much about the military training he received, but the instilling of Nazi doctrine and ideology, with the main focus being on anti-Semitism.

Despite successfully completing the course it would be a further two years before he became a member of the Nazi Party, an event which, although he was extremely proud of it at the time, wasn't something he was happy to admit to in a post-war Germany.

Incidentally, one of the instructors on Peiper's course was Sturmbannführer Franz Magill who later led the SS Cavalry Regiment 2 during Operation Barbarossa. During August and September 1941, Magill and his men were in the city of Pinsk, which is now part of Belarus; they helped in the round up of all men aged between 18 and 55, resulting in up to 8,000 men being shot. A further 2,000 women, children and older men were also murdered.

In February 1943 Magill oversaw Operation Hornung, the destruction of the ghetto in the city of Sluck, also now in modern-day Belarus.

Franz Magill was the deputy commander of the Special Battalion Dirlewanger, who issued the following order:

> The battalion is to again comb through the combat zone of February 15 to February 17 up to the line Starobin-Powarczycze. Everything that may give shelter or protection is to be destroyed. The area is to become no man's land. All inhabitants are to be shot. Cattle, grain and other products are to be taken and delivered to Starobin. The Russian company is to go back into the combat zone and destroy everything and lead the cattle out in a northerly direction. The sled column is to be kept so far from the location to be destroyed that the civilian drivers are not present at the executions.

After having successfully passed his course, Peiper received the prized posting he was hoping for, that of the Leibstandarte SS Adolf Hitler, where he remained until June 1938. Peiper's popularity was most definitely on the rise, and a young man that Himmler had most definitely not forgotten about. At 23 years of age, Peiper's next 'posting' saw him become an adjutant to Himmler, indicating the potential he believed the young Peiper had to become a high ranking member of the SS.

A common theme which appeared to have followed Peiper throughout his SS career, especially in his early years of service, was the number of the high ranking SS and Nazi officials he came in to contact with, men he either served with or under, or were his instructors. Whilst working for Himmler for example, Peiper met another such individual.

When Peiper took up his position as adjutant, the chief of Himmler's Personal Staff Reichsführer-SS, and the SS liaison officer with Adolf Hitler, was SS-Obergruppenführer Karl Friedrich Otto Wolf, a man who was also Himmler's 'eyes and ears' within Hitler's headquarters.

It was later proved that Wolf was complicit in the murder of 300,000 Jews, yet despite his involvement in the Holocaust he was not prosecuted at the post-war Nuremberg trials. This was because of his direct involvement in Operation Sunshine, a number of secret meetings which took place between February and May 1945, to arrange a local surrender of all German forces in northern Italy, with most of the meetings actually taking place in Bern, Switzerland, between Wolf and Allen Dulles, an agent of the American Office of Strategic Services. Part of the discussions apparently involved a verbal agreement by Dulles to protect Wolf from prosecution at any post-war trials if the surrender became a reality. If such an agreement was made, it shows just how much the Americans wanted the surrender to go ahead before Italian communists could gain any kind of control in the region.

The question here is, did Dulles make such a promise with the support and approval of President Roosevelt, or was it simply a decision he made to ensure that the proposed surrender of German forces actually went ahead?

How much contact Peiper had with Wolf is unclear, but Wolf would have undoubtedly been aware of Himmler's liking of the young Peiper.

The position of adjutant to someone such as Himmler was most definitely a game changer for a young man wanting to cut out a career for himself in the SS, and the longer that position was held, the better it would be for the individual concerned because it would bring with it both political influence and connections. This was the world that Peiper now found himself in.

It was while working for Himmler that Peiper met his future wife, Sigurd Hinrichsen, who was one of the secretaries on Himmler's personal staff. This liaison unintentionally opened up even more connections as Sigurd was good friends with Lina Heydrich, the wife of the Chief of the Reich Main Security Office, Reinhard Heydrich, and Hedwig Potthast, rumoured to be Himmler's mistress.

Peiper and Sigurd married in Berlin on 26 June 1939, with the guest of honour at their wedding being none other than Heinrich Himmler.

The relationship between Himmler and Peiper had not waned any by the outbreak of the Second World War, which for Peiper could only be a good thing. Being favoured by a man of Himmler's position and power within the Nazi Party was a massive positive for anybody wanting to rise through the ranks of the SS. To have him as an enemy would have been potentially life threatening, which raises the question, did you have to be a 'yes man' in his presence and company, or did he surround himself with individuals whom he knew would challenge him in an appropriate and acceptable manner? Was Himmler the type of individual who liked and respected a frank answer, or did he want to hear only what he wanted to hear? Either way, I do not have the impression that Peiper was a 'yes man' to those senior to him in rank.

On 1 September 1939, German forces invaded Poland, with Himmler making his way there on his special train, Sonderzug Steiermark, and Joachim Peiper was one of those accompanying him. Although plush by comparison to civilian trains, it was poorly equipped for military purposes. It only had one telephone line and no radio system, preventing the ability to communicate orders to troops on the ground.

What becomes apparent when researching Peiper, and many other Nazis for that matter, is how commonplace and 'normal' death and murder became. On the surface these men appear to have absolutely no empathy for those they choose to murder for no real reason, other than because they could.

On 13 December 1939, Peiper accompanied Himmler on a visit to a psychiatric facility located in the Polish village of Owinska, seven miles north of Poznan. There he witnessed the murder by gassing of a number of the facility's residents. Seven years later, while being interrogated by the Americans, he speaks of that day as if he was telling his wife about his day at work before sitting down to eat his dinner.

> The action (gassing) was done before a circle of invited guests. … The insane were lead in to a prepared casement, the door of which had a Plexiglas window. After the door was closed, one could see how, in the beginning, the insane still laughed and talked to each other. But, soon they sat down on the straw, obviously under the influence of the gas. … Very soon, they no longer moved.

Other than being instructed to by Himmler, why would anybody want, or need, to witness such an atrocity against human life, especially as there could be no benefit whatsoever gained from watching such an unfortunate group of individuals murdered in cold blood.

Although he may not have appreciated it at the time, Peiper was deeply involved in the development of SS policies concerning the 'ethnic cleansing' of the Polish population, something he witnessed at first hand. But his involvement didn't end there. Any later claim he might have made about not knowing of the Holocaust would have been easy for an interrogator to disprove. During the first couple of months of 1940, he had accompanied Himmler on a tour of Nazi concentration camps, which included Neuengamme and Sachsenhausen.

Neuengamme was actually a network of concentration camps that were located in the Bergedorf district of Hamburg, and consisted of Neuengamme and a staggering eighty-five satellite camps, twenty-four of which were purely for women. Neuengamme was first opened in 1938 and remained in use as a concentration camp through to the end of the war. At the war's end it was, ironically, used by the British Army as an internment camp for members of the SS and Nazi officials.

During its existence, more than 100,000 prisoners spent time at Neuengamme and its satellite camps, of which it is estimated nearly 43,000 died or were killed. This figure includes more than 16,000 who died either on death marches that had set off from the main camp, or during an RAF bombing raid on four ships on which prisoners from the camps had been placed. More than 7,000 prisoners were killed during the raid, which was carried out because the RAF wrongly believed the ships contained escaping Nazis. Some of those who managed to escape from the ships' holds and jump in to the sea were machine-gunned by Nazi officials aboard the vessels, and by the RAF aircraft who still believed they were firing upon Nazis.

As for Sachsenhausen, it was a Nazi concentration camp which had first opened in 1936, and was mainly used to hold political prisoners, including some very prominent ones such as Yakov Iosifovich Dzhugashvili, the elder son of Soviet leader, Joseph Stalin, who had been captured during Operation Barbarossa, on 16 July 1941.

Official German documents captured by the British after the war show that Dzhugashvili died on 14 April 1943, when he ran in to one of the camps electric fences and was shot. An autopsy carried out by the Germans recorded that he had died of electrocution before being shot, whether this was actually the case, we will never know.

Another prominent prisoner held at Sachsenhausen was Paul Reynaud, the penultimate Prime Minister of the French Third Republic, who found himself incarcerated there in 1942.

Ultimately, Sachsenhausen was a labour camp, but it still had a gas chamber, and was also used by Nazi doctors to carry out medical experiments.

Looking at photographs of Peiper during these times, and especially when he was accompanying Himmler on official visits, regardless of where they were, he quite often looks pretty vacant or distant, like he isn't really interested in being there. He has the look a person has just before they glance at their watch to see what the time is, so that they can work out how much longer they have to endure.

In April 1940, Himmler continued his tour of Nazi Germany's concentration camps, and once again Peiper was by his side like an obedient and faithful puppy. The tour also included a visit to Lublin in Poland, where they met with the city's SS and Police Leader, Odilo Globocnik. The reason for the meeting and topic of conversation concerned how to conduct the murder of large numbers of people, whose only 'crime' was to be disabled. As I type these words, I am struggling to understand just how that conversation would have gone. How could any sane individual, or group of individuals, sit down and calmly have such a conversation over a cup of tea. Even if one of them was mad, surely all of them could not have been. Surely at least one of them was sat there thinking to themselves, 'what are we doing having such a conversation. This is madness.' Apparently not.

Himmler and Peiper had previously met with Globocnik when their topic of conversation had been the deportation of Jews from German controlled areas of Poland to the Jewish ghettos in Warsaw and Lublin.

Because of Peiper's history and connections with the high-powered individuals who had been involved in his life, including his own father, his political views were such that I doubt he would have been shocked or disgusted by any of the topics of conversation. I find it hard to believe, however, that this is how he would have wanted to spend the rest of the war, by attending meetings and conferences, and having conversations on the best way to murder civilian populations.

At the beginning of the Battle of France in May 1940, he once again found himself by Himmler's side as they followed troops of the Waffen-SS. This proved to be an extremely frustrating experience for a young Joachim Peiper, who wanted to be in on the action. If he was to have any credibility among his fellow officers and the men that he would undoubtedly lead, he needed hands-on fighting experience. Being Himmler's adjutant would 'open certain doors' and bring with it a certain amount of fear, but not respect. He knew that if he wanted respect, he would have to earn it by getting his hands dirty. He also realised that knowing the theory on how to fight a battle would only take a man so far, but quite often theory and reality turned out to be totally different.

Peiper pleaded with Himmler to allow him the opportunity to gain some combat experience, which he agreed to. Peiper linked up with the LSSAH as a platoon leader and was quickly in the thick of the fighting. His opportunity for military action was short lived, only lasting from 18 May to 21 June 1940, but it was long enough to show his true capabilities as a 'hands-on soldier'. For his actions in that relatively short period of time, he was promoted to the rank of SS-Hauptsturmführer and awarded the Iron Cross both 2nd and 1st Class. An amazing achievement by any stretch of the imagination. It had also provided him with the hands-on battle experience he had so desired, and a credibility in the eyes of his fellow officers and troops alike.

With the excitement and experience of battle tucked neatly under his belt, he returned to his day job as adjutant to Himmler. It could not have been so far removed from what he had spent the previous month doing.

Although Operation Barbarossa was not activated until 22 June 1941, Peiper had been told about it by Himmler in February the same year, such was the trust he had in him. A week before it began, both men attended a five-day conference concerning the forthcoming invasion. One of the topics of conversation was the plan to eliminate some 30 million Slavic people. This was part of what was known by the Germans as Generalplan Ost.

The intended way for these killings to take place was a combination of mass shootings by groups such as the Einsatzgruppen and a programme of starvation, for Nazi Germany to be able to colonise central and eastern Europe. Germany was so confident of winning the war they had even split their plan in to two parts. The first part, known as the Kleine Planung (the 'Small Plan'), covered actions that were to take place during the course of the war. The second part, the Grosse Planung (the 'Big Plan'), would be more gradual and take anything between twenty-five to thirty years to complete.

Bialystock is the largest city in northeast Poland, and in July 1941, it was the focus for the murder of large numbers of Polish Jews, atrocities which were carried out by members of the Order Police battalions, the Kommandostab Reichführer-SS, and elements of the Einsatzgruppen.

The Order Police battalions were utilised in German occupied areas under German civilian administration. In essence, their job was to murder members of the Jewish population in areas where they were deployed.

The Kommandostab Reichsführer-SS was a paramilitary unit that was part of the SS, and came under the direct control of Himmler. It was the Kommandostab units who reported to Himmler's office the figures for Jews they had killed the previous day. The man tasked with the responsibility of receiving this information was none other than Joachim Peiper, which meant that from a relatively early stage of the war, he was well aware of the atrocities and murders that were being perpetrated against the Jewish people.

Once Peiper was in possession of this information, he in turn had to present it, along with similar information which he received from the Einsatzgruppen, to Himmler every morning for his perusal. These reports would include words such as 'looters', a euphemism for 'Jews', and terminology such as 'cleansing action', which was a reference to 'shootings'.

What really struck me about this is how Peiper managed to reconcile the knowledge and information he was privy to as Himmler's adjutant, concerning the number of murders that were being perpetrated by the Nazis throughout Poland, of men, women and children, Catholic and Jewish alike, with the fact that he was a married man and a father.

In *Joachim Peiper: A Biography of Himmler's SS Commander*, Jens Westemeir explains how available archived German records show that Peiper and Himmler parted company in October 1941, when the former transferred to the LSSAH, although the pair remained in touch and on good terms throughout the war years.

Although Peiper had been a member of the Nazi Party since 1934, this was the turning point, in both his life and career, which saw the change from being just another name in the history of the Second World War, to somebody who was remembered for the cold-blooded murder of innocent citizens and the massacre of unarmed American prisoners of war. A man the Nazi propaganda machine turned in to a war hero, pin-up boy, and an example of what a 'real life' German fighting man should be, and what America wanted to demonise as a cold and heartless monster, who could take a life in the blink of an eye.

When Peiper rejoined the LSSAH, he took command of its 11th Company, which was involved in fighting on the Eastern Front, specifically Mariupol, which today is part of the Ukraine, which was occupied by German forces between 8 October 1941 and 10 September 1943. During this period, the city's entire Jewish population was murdered.

Peiper and his men were also involved in fighting in Rostov-on-Don, which today is a port city in Russia. German forces occupied the city twice during the war; the first time was between 19 November and 2 December 1941, when elements of the German 1st Panzer Army, which would have included Peiper and his men, were forced out of the city when the 37th Army, commanded by Lieutenant-General Anton Ivanovich Lopatin, counter-attacked them from the north

Peiper quickly gained a reputation as being a daring and audacious fighter, who did not shy away from confrontation, and certainly was not a man prone to retreat. This was all well and good for him personally, but it led to very high casualty rates among his men, and left him open to allegations that he cared more about enhancing his personal reputation than he did about the welfare of his men. But despite this, those who survived were fiercely loyal to him, with many of them regarding him as a 'charismatic' leader.

During the second occupation, between 23 July 1942 and 14 February 1943, some 30,000 Jews and Russian civilians were massacred by German forces of Einsatzguppe D, at Zmiyovskaya Balka, which was the largest single site of murdered Jews anywhere in Russia during the course of the war. Although Einstazgruppe D had been following behind Peiper and his men, 11th Company had left the Eastern Front at this point and was in France from May 1942, for vehicle refitting and repair, and for the officers and men to have a period of rest and recuperation. This meant that they could not have been involved in the murder of the 30,000 Jews and Russian civilians.

While back in France, Peiper took the opportunity to rekindle his friendship with Himmler, meeting with him on more than one occasion both formally and informally. Also while in France, the Leiberstandarte SS-Adolf Hitler, was changed to a mechanized infantry division, or Panzergrenadier, where infantry troops were transported in combat vehicles. Peiper was promoted and placed in command of the newly formed 3rd (Armoured Personnel Carrier) Battalion, Leibstandarte's 2nd Panzer Grenadier Regiment, who returned to the Eastern Front in January 1943, at a time when things were not going according Hitler's plans.

Chapter Three

Peiper's Killings – 1943

It was during the course of 16 and 17 February 1943 that the propensity for wanton murder appears to have begun for Joachim Peiper and his men.

SS troops under the command of Joachim Peiper occupied the villages of Yefremovka and Semyonovka on 12 February 1943. Four days later, on the morning of 16 February, a German aircraft carrying some high ranking SS officers landed near the village of Semyonovka and was fired upon by either partisans or Soviet soldiers. Two SS officers were wounded in the shooting. In retaliation, that same evening Peiper is alleged to have ordered the destruction of the two villages and the killing of all of the inhabitants. Monuments in these two villages apparently record the names of 872 local men, women and children who were murdered by Peiper's men between 16 and 17 February 1943, but this figure could be higher if men from other nearby locations were in either of the villages at the time. Of those killed, 240 of them were men who were locked in the village church at Yefremovka, which was then set on fire. There were no survivors.

As with many such events during the Second World War, it is extremely difficult to establish the exact facts of what happened. Both sides in such events will obviously provide different and conflicting versions of what took place, and there are rarely any survivors among those who were killed. A 14-year-old boy named Ivan Vasil'yevich Kiselev, who lived at 1, Grigori Alekseevich, Buznyka, is reported to have witnessed soldiers from the LSSAH carry out this atrocity, but I am unclear how it would have been possible for him to have been present at both massacres and to identify who was responsible, regardless of how likely it is that one group of soldiers carried out both. Undoubtedly, while the killings were being carried out Kiselev would have been hiding, because if German soldiers had discovered him, he also would have been killed.

It was during the Third Battle of Kharkov between 19 February and 15 March 1943, that Peiper's desire to continue his murderous ways once again overcame him. It was also for his actions during this battle that he was awarded Germany's highest military decoration, the Knight's Cross of the Iron Cross with Oak Leaves and Swords, more commonly known as simply the Knight's Cross.

During the battle, and despite orders to the contrary, Peiper who was in charge of the 3rd Battalion, 2nd Panzergrenadier Regiment, pushed some thirty miles through enemy lines to reach the German 320th Infantry Division, who had become encircled by Soviet forces. Eventually, after a fierce battle, they defeated the Soviets, believed to be soldiers from an elite ski battalion, and entered the village looking for twenty-five comrades who had been part of a rearguard medical detachment. It wasn't long before they found them, but there was no euphoria or congratulations because every single one of them was dead. Those responsible had not only seen fit to kill the captured German soldiers, but had mutilated them as well. The only hope for these poor souls was that they had been killed before they had been mutilated. One account states that their genitalia had been cut off and their eyes gouged out. Fighting on the Eastern Front during Operation Barbarossa was brutal, with little or no quarter being given by either side, and there was rarely any adherence to the rules of engagement as laid down by the terms of the Geneva Convention when it came to the treatment of enemy prisoners of war.

Peiper was enraged with the acts of brutality which had been perpetrated on his men. Not knowing if the murders had been carried out by partisans or Russian soldiers, his response was swift. In *Hitler's Warrior: The Life and Wars of SS Colonel Jochen Peiper* by Danny S. Parker, it is mentioned that as revenge, Peiper orders his men to torch the entire village and kill every single man, woman and child, which they proceed to do.

When it was time to begin the return journey, there was no way of knowing what or who they would encounter. Leading from the front, Peiper and his men made their way to the Udy River, only to discover that their onward journey had been cut off by Soviet forces who had destroyed the river's main bridge.

Undeterred, Peiper and his men fought their way through the streets of the city, eventually arriving at what had been the entrance to the bridge, which they then proceeded to repair as quickly as they could. This was sufficient enough for the ambulances that were carrying wounded men and officers of the 320th Infantry Division to cross and make good their escape. But the newly repaired bridge was nowhere strong enough to take the weight of Peiper's heavily armoured half-tracks, meaning he and his men had to remain behind Soviet lines and find another route back to safety, which they eventually managed to do.

Peiper was awarded the Knight's Cross on 9 March 1943, and even received the personal congratulations of his old boss, Heinrich Himmler: 'Heartfelt congratulations for the Knights Cross my dear Jochen. I am proud of you.'

The D-Day landings of June 1944, and the Allied invasion of Nazi-occupied Europe, placed German forces under considerable strain. They had spent large periods of 1941, '42 and '43 trying their best to conquer the Soviet Union, but with a costly defeat at Stalingrad in 1942, and a more damning one at the Battle of Kursk in 1943, they were nowhere near the force they had once been. Germany had some 4 million men killed in action fighting against Soviet forces and they lost a further 370,000 men who had been captured and taken as prisoners of war, but died whilst in captivity. With Soviet forces already attacking them from the East, they now had to contend with Allied forces gaining a foothold in German-occupied France.

With Adolf Hitler now requiring large numbers of men to hold back the ever-increasing numbers of American, British and Commonwealth troops landing on the beaches of Normandy, Joachim Peiper and his men of Kampfgruppe (Combat Group) Peiper, which consisted of some 140 tanks and a battalion of motorised infantry, were sent to the Western Front to help out. After almost three years of nearly non-stop fighting, Peiper was also beginning to feel the strain. He was physically exhausted, and psychologically, all the fighting, death and killing had started to take their toll on him.

In the summer of 1944, the German High Command let it be known that Peiper was suffering from jaundice and required a period of medical attention. The reality was possibly somewhat different. The rumour was that he had actually suffered a nervous breakdown, not something that the German authorities could ever allow to become common knowledge. He was their poster boy, the ultimate embodiment of a German warrior. If word spread about that he might have had a nervous breakdown, it could have had a devastating effect on the morale of the entire German war effort, along with the men of the German armed forces. By December 1944, and the Battle of the Bulge, he had recovered sufficiently to resume his command of Kampfgruppe Peiper, with none of his men any the wiser about what had really happened to him.

There remains some confusion over what actually happened to Peiper, and also when it happened, as other reports mention it taking place after the Battle of the Bulge. A medical file on Peiper is held in the United States National Archives, but most of it relates to his time held as a prisoner at Landsberg Prison in Germany in the years after the war. It is known that Peiper had a weak heart, but how badly that affected his overall health is unclear. It certainly did not prevent him from being on active service during the war. What would have made matters worse for him is that he was a heavy smoker, and drank a lot of coffee, meaning his caffeine intake was extremely high. He also had very low blood pressure, which sometimes resulted in him passing out.

Another aspect worth some consideration is what he would have been experiencing in an emotional sense. He was heavily involved in the Battle of the Bulge, which saw the Germans defeated, basically because they didn't have enough men to cope with the scale of the opposition.

In their initial attack Germany deployed more than 400,000 men, some 1,200 tanks, tank destroyers and assault guns, along with 4,224 artillery pieces. During the battle they received reinforcements of around 50,000 men. It is believed that Germany lost up to 100,000 men, either killed, wounded, missing or captured and taken as prisoners of war. They were up against a combined Allied force of more than 610,000 men.

Peiper sustained a bullet wound to his left hand during the Battle of the Bulge in December 1944, in addition to a shrapnel splinter to one of his thighs sustained at Normandy in July 1944. He hadn't had much sleep throughout the battle, which at one stage saw him awake for more than twenty-four hours, and he and his men were heavily implicated in allegations of war crimes. He was exhausted, depressed and suffering a wound, albeit a relatively minor one. He received treatment at a medical facility at Verbandplatz, in Wanne, Germany, where he spent much of the time sleeping. He also spent time at both the Corps hospital at Sees and the Tegersee Reserve Hospital at Lake Tegern, Bavaria.

A document dated 30 January 1945 lists Peiper's nine wounds and illnesses and is signed by the SS Regimental Doctor, Stickel. The first entry relates to 1940, two more were in 1941, one was in 1942, there were four in 1944, and one in 1945. The document is typed in German and the only version I could find was not clear enough for accurate translation.

German Doctor Kurt Stickel had treated Peiper on more than one occasion, and in one report he wrote that Peiper had suffered from Cholecystitis, which relates to gallstones. As one of the symptoms is severe pain under the ribcage, initially it could have been considered that Peiper was having a heart attack.

All of these elements added together, along with the extreme stress he must have been under, are good ingredients for a breakdown, the question is which – a nervous or physical one?

Despite the fact that Peiper was an extremely brave individual, his medical record also shows that despite attempts by the German propaganda machine to make him out to be a 'superhero' to whom every German male should aspire, he was also just the same as everyone else: a vulnerable individual prone to a number of ailments, both physical and mental.

Chapter Four

Boves Massacre

Boves is a town situated in the north west of Italy close to the border with France. In July 1943, after the Allied invasion of Sicily, the Fascist Italian leader Benito Mussolini was deposed and placed under arrest. What remained of his government collapsed.

The Italian King, Victor Emanuel, asked General Pietro Badoglio to replace Mussolini. Soon after taking up his position, Badoglio began negotiations with America about an acceptable surrender.

On 8 September 1943, General Dwight D. Eisenhower announced the unconditional surrender of all Italian forces to the Allies. As part of the agreement, Allied troops landed unopposed the following day at Salerno as part of Operation Avalanche.

The same day as Eisenhower announced Italy's surrender, Hitler launched Operation Axis, his plan to occupy Italy. There were two reasons for this: first, if the Allies took the whole of Italy, they would be in easy reach of the German occupied Balkan states; and second, Hitler did not want Italian naval vessels falling in to the hands of the Allies.

The Italian surrender saw a number of their troops returning to Italy from France, via Boves and the surrounding area. This was a real concern for Germany. With such a large number of returning Italian troops pouring into the country, the worry was they might decide to join the Italian partisans.

Joachim Peiper and the men of the 1st Panzer Division, LSSAH, were stationed in the same region, their orders were to take control of the border area in and around Boves. With the Allies having already begun their invasion of Italy in the south, and the build-up of Italian partisans throughout the country, the Germans had enough to worry about. In the circumstances, the arrest and detention of Jews was the last thing on their mind and was most certainly not a priority. For some unbeknown reason, Peiper and his men did exactly that, which was not something they had been instructed to do. They also carried out acts of looting of Jewish homes and businesses, and actively sought out any Jewish people they could find, even after they had been explicitly told not to by the SS corps commander, General Paul Hauser.

As with all such war-time incidents, it is not always possible to ascertain the exact truth about what actually took place. Sometimes it isn't possible because there are two different versions of the same events, one from each opposing side, and sometimes it is simply because there were no surviving witnesses.

What is known about the Boves massacre is that it took place on 19 December 1943, and came about after two German soldiers were captured by a group of Italians, some of whom were regular Italian soldiers while others were partisans.

The Germans' initial decision was simple and straightforward: 'let's go and get our men back'. But the attempt by a company of SS men of the Leibstandarte not only failed, but resulted in one of them being killed and a number being wounded, along with one of the Italians also being killed. What ensued in the immediate aftermath was a stand-off situation. It was at this stage that Peiper and his men were called upon to resolve the situation. They quickly sealed off the entry and access points in and out of the town, and sent a message that unless the two German soldiers were released, the town would be destroyed and all those in it killed. He agreed not to carry out either threat if the men were released. Negotiations between the two sides were carried out through don Giuseppi Bernardi, Boves' parish priest, and a local businessman, Alessandro Vassallo.

The negotiations worked; the two German soldiers were released unharmed and the body of the dead German soldier was also returned. Now was the time to see if Peiper was as good as his word. He was not. The priest and the businessman had petrol poured over them, were set on fire and died an agonising death as they were burned alive.

This was just the beginning. Peiper further reneged on his promises when he sent his men in to the village to destroy homes and kill its inhabitants. By the time it was over twenty-three unarmed, innocent civilians had been murdered and some 350 homes in the village had been set on fire and destroyed. Worse still, if that is possible, all those who were killed were either elderly, sick or bedridden because everybody who could leave, including the partisans and Italian soldiers, had already gone before the massacre began, and had made their way up in to the surrounding hills and mountains.

The following piece was taken from an article about the massacre which appears on Wikipedia, collectively compiled from a number of Italian websites which I have included in my source material.

> Among the victims was Bartolomeo Ghinamo, a deaf mute living in Via Vigne, who was gunned down when he tried to put out a fire after Peiper's men had set his house afire; Francesco Dalmasso, a

> disabled veteran, who was shot dead while trying to escape through the fields; Caterina Bo, an 87-year-old woman who could not move from her bed, was burned alive when Peiper's men set fire to her house. The deputy parish priest, don Mario Ghibaudo, was killed while giving absolution to an old man who had been shot by a German soldier. Adriana Masino, an inhabitant of Boves, testified to Colonel Chiorando on 12 January 1968 (during Peiper's trial) that she and her brother Giacomo were dragging a cart through a street when they met two German soldiers; they raised their hands and Giacomo moved towards them saying that he could speak two languages. One of the two soldiers made a gesture to the other, and Giacomo Masino was shot dead on the spot. Michel and Piero Sopra, when testifying to the military chaplain, Luigi Feltrin for the identification of don Mario Ghibaudo's body, stated that they too were fleeing from the village when they met some German soldiers; one of them shot Michele Agnese, their grandfather in the head. Don Ghibaudo gave Agnese the absolution and was shot dead in turn. This happened around 18:00 in Via Badina. Giacomo Dalmasso, a 29-year-old cart driver, was shot multiple times but survived after 93 days in hospital, as the bullets did not hit any vital organs.

It is staggering to think that, even in such times, men who had been civilised human beings before the war could act in such a barbaric and savage manner to innocent civilians who posed no threat to them whatsoever.

Men like Peiper use words such as 'honour' to describe the camaraderie they had between each other, and the way they fought in battle, yet they were completely at ease with breaking their promises once they had been given what they wanted, and not just killing innocent civilians, but burning them alive. It is difficult to see how such actions can, in all sensibility, ever include the word 'honour'.

After the war Peiper justified the killing of civilians as collateral damage in a war action. What he did not clarify was whether he was referring to individuals who were members of the 'partisans' or the 'resistance movement'; innocent peoples of the Jewish faith; unarmed civilians; just some or all of these.

If any Italian soldiers were uncertain about what they should do next, having returned home after Italy's surrender to the Allies, I believe the barbaric murder of twenty-three innocent civilians, and fellow Italians at Boves, would have gone a long way to making their minds up for them. The ranks of the

Italian Partisan movement would, no doubt, have increased considerably after September 1943.

Remarkably, neither Peiper nor any of his men were prosecuted for the massacre at Boves in any war crimes' trials after the war. In 1968, twenty-five years after the Boves massacres, some of the survivors attempted to have Peiper and two of the men who served under him, Lieutenants Otto Heinrich Dinse and Erhard Guhrs, convicted for their actions at Boves; an Italian court decided there was 'insufficient suspicion of criminal activity on the part of any of the accused to warrant prosecution'.

In post-war Germany, authorities carried out their own investigations into any related wartime crimes which were believed to have been carried out by German military personnel. Where sufficient evidence was discovered to charge individuals with a war crime, they did so.

At the District Court in Stuttgart on 23 December 1968, in the case of Joachim Peiper and the surviving members of his unit, the German authorities reached the same conclusion as the Italian court, that there was insufficient evidence to prosecute anybody in connection with the Boves massacre of September 1943.

Although this book focuses on Joachim Peiper and the atrocities he and his men carried out during the course of the Second World War, the atrocity at Boves provides the opportunity to show just how widespread the massacre of innocent civilians, or unarmed prisoners of war actually was – and not just by German forces.

There were other massacres of Italian civilians by members of the German SS during 1943, but Allied forces also carried out similar attacks.

I believe this demonstrates how men fighting on either side during the war, who were just normal, everyday people, living a law abiding existence prior to the war, could change so quickly and easily and become cold-blooded, unemotional killers.

On 14 July 1943, during the Allied invasion of Sicily, men of the United States 180th Infantry Regiment were tasked with capturing the Santo Pietro airfield at Biscari. Once there, they came up against stiff opposition from a combined German/Italian force, but during the early exchanges the Americans captured forty-five Italians and three Germans soldiers. A group of American soldiers were then ordered by Major Roger Denman, the executive officer of the Regiment's 1st Battalion, to take the prisoners to the rear for questioning. After marching the prisoners for about a mile, Sergeant Horace T. West, stopped the group, separated nine of the prisoners for interrogation, before opening fire on the remaining prisoners with a Thompson sub-machine gun. By the time he had finished, thirty-seven of them were dead. During the incident, having run out of ammunition, he had calmly loaded a second magazine.

After this first massacre had taken place, men of 'C' Company, 1st Battalion, 180th Infantry Regiment, led by Captain John T. Compton, also arrived at the Santo Pietro airfield at Biscari, and quickly found themselves under enemy fire, which included some accurate and deadly sniper fire. Compton and his men were able to establish the general direction from which the sniper-fire was coming, but were unable to establish an exact location or whether there was more than one sniper.

The sniper-fire had been so accurate that a dozen of Compton's men were either wounded or killed. Another of Compton's men, Private Raymond C. Marlow, crept out from his position to see if he could locate the sniper, which he did. He shouted at the man, who was dressed in an Italian army uniform, but the man turned and ran a short distance before disappearing into a dugout. Marlow followed but stayed a safe distance away from the dugout; much to his surprise, after only a couple of minutes, the man reappeared with his hands in the air, along with a further thirty-five of his colleagues, some of whom were wearing civilian clothing. Marlow escorted his newly acquired prisoners back to his position, where Marlow's fellow Private, John Gazzetti, who was of Italian descent and spoke the language, asked them if they had been acting as snipers, but received no reply.

All Private Marlow wanted to know was what he should do with his prisoners. The young and relatively inexperienced 1st Lieutenant Blanks asked Compton what he wanted doing with the prisoners; in reply Compton asked Blanks if the prisoners had been the same ones who had been sniping on them throughout the day. Inexcusably, Blanks said that they had been, despite not knowing that to be the case. On hearing this Compton ordered the men to be shot. Compton took part in the shooting of the Italian prisoners, telling his men before the firing began, 'I don't want to see a man left standing when the firing is done.' Every one of the Italian prisoners was killed.

News of the two massacres eventually reached General Omar Bradley, who was the commander of the United States ll Corps during the Allied invasion of Sicily, who in turn spoke with General George Patton on the matter. Patton noted in his diary:

> I told Bradley it was probably an exaggeration, but in any case to tell the Officer to certify that the dead men were snipers or had attempted to escape or something, as it would make a stink in the

> press and also would make the civilians mad. Anyhow, they are dead, so nothing can be done about it.

It would be fair to say that Bradley did not agree with Patton's suggestions. A subsequent American investigation found that the Italians had been unlawfully shot dead by American soldiers without any provocation.

Both Sergeant West and Captain Compton faced court martials. In their defence, the two men both claimed that they were following orders given by their commanding officer. This was confirmed by Colonel Forrest E. Cookson, who was West's regimental commander, and gave evidence to the effect that the commanding officer, who just happened to be General George Patton, had said that if the enemy continued to resist after US troops had come within 200 yards of their defensive positions, surrender of those enemy soldiers need not be accepted. Even if Patton had made such a statement, which he later denied, in both cases the enemy combatants who were murdered were unarmed prisoners of war at the time they were killed, so the defence of 'I was simply carrying out the orders of my commanding officer', went out the window.

In the case of West, he was found guilty of premeditated murder, reduced to the ranks and sentenced to life imprisonment.

The American military authorities hadn't, up to that point in time, ducked the issue, but the case was undoubtedly a problem. They did the right thing in the first place by putting West on trial, and then did even better by coming up with the correct outcome. But that was where it became a real problem for them because they had not made the proceedings public knowledge through concern of the reaction the case would receive both back in America, as well as throughout Italy. The American people believed they were on the side of right and good, despite being involved in a war with which some of them did not agree, because for them it was a European war and one they shouldn't have been involved with in the first place. Knowing that one of their own was actually one of the very monsters they believed they were fighting against, might well have caused an adverse effect in areas such as recruitment, or even the desire to continue their involvement in the war. In Italy, it could have been a real problem. If word of the incident had spread, it could have acted as a call to arms for the Italian soldiers who had laid them down when their country had surrendered. Then the Allies could have once again found themselves fighting against the Italian Army.

In the circumstances, the American authorities could not run the risk of sending West home and placing him in an American prison, because if they did, who he was and what he had done would most definitely leak out. Instead he was incarcerated in a military prison out of the way in North Africa.

Just one year later, everything changed. West's brother back in America had found out what had happened, and written to both his Senator as well as the army concerning his brother. The United States War Department's Bureau of Public Relations, concerned that the matter might reach the ears of the national newspapers if West's brother made too much of an issue about the case, recommended that it would be best for all concerned if West's sentence was remitted. So it was that on 24 November 1944, the Deputy Commander of Allied Forces in Italy, Dwight D. Eisenhower, signed the order of remittance in West's case.

Despite being a convicted mass murderer, West remained in the army and continued to see service during the remaining months of the war. Even more remarkable was the fact that when he was demobbed on his eventual return to the United States he received an honourable discharge.

I believe that part of the reason he was allowed to remain in the army and resume his military career during the war was the hope by American military authorities that he would be killed in action.

In the case of Captain Compton, the outcome was somewhat different. At his court martial he was charged with the pre-meditated murder of thirty-six enemy prisoners of war under his control. In his defence, he too stated that he was simply following the orders given to him by his commanding officer. He also claimed *respondeat superior*, which in simple terms means that senior officers who gave orders which were clearly in breach of international law, and who then failed in their responsibility to prevent such acts from being carried out, are also criminally liable.

Remarkably, Compton was acquitted of the charges against him on 23 October 1943, a decision possibly swayed by the desire to avoid prosecuting a senior officer, which in Compton's case would have been General Patton. Despite the fact that a Judge Advocate's review of the case found that Compton had acted unlawfully, he was released and transferred to the United States 179th Infantry Regiment, who had the nickname of the 'Tomahawks'. Just two weeks after his acquittal he was killed in action on 8 November 1943, while serving in Italy. The 179th saw action in Sicily, Naples, Anzio, and Rome during their time in Italy.

Just six weeks after carrying out the massacre at Boves, Peiper and his men were again serving on the Eastern Front.

Chapter Five

The Ardenne Abbey Massacre

In June 1944, twenty Canadian soldiers were captured and murdered by the Waffen SS at Normandy in what became known as the Ardenne Abbey Massacre.

All the available evidence shows that this atrocity had nothing to do with Joachim Peiper and the men under his control. The man responsible was in fact SS Standartenführer Kurt Meyer, who was in command of the 25th Panzer Grenadier Regiment, along with what has been described as the 'fanatical' 12th Panzer Division Hitlerjugend.

The reason for including this story is the SS Panzer connection, which raises the question whether these men were both psychopaths who had no empathy with humanity, or were they simply carrying out orders from a higher authority within the German military.

With the war in what would be its final year, the massacres at Malmedy, Wereth and at Ardenne Abbey, took place within six months of each other, albeit in different countries and more than 350 miles apart, but this showed just how widespread and entrenched the mindset of SS forces could be.

A group of twenty Canadian soldiers serving with the North Nova Scotia Highlanders and the 27th Armoured Regiment, which was part of the Sherbrooke Fusilier Regiment were captured near Caen in northwest France, and massacred in the Ardenne Abbey. By the summer of 1944, many of the officers and soldiers who made up the SS units were experienced and battle-hardened men who had seen action in, and fought their way across, Poland, Belgium and France. To them, death was nothing new. Many of them had lived with it as an almost constant companion, and this had taught them how to put aside any personal emotions about killing.

Like Peiper, Meyer was an ardent Nazi, and had been a member since 1930, three years before Hitler and the Nazi Party came to power.

In battle he did not shirk responsibility but did what needed to be done, which gained him a reputation as being an excellent soldier. But he just as quickly gained a more notorious reputation as being somebody who was more than willing to murder the civilians and unarmed prisoners of war he and his men had captured.

In contrast to him and his men, the Canadian soldiers murdered in the Ardennes Abbey were young men, with absolutely no previous combat experience, and who had only arrived in Europe on D-Day, 6 June 1944, when they had come ashore at Juno Beach, Normandy. They were either shot or bludgeoned to death the following evening, 7 June.

They were murdered at Ardenne Abbey because it was the headquarters of the 25th Panzer Grenadier Regiment, and was where they were taken after being captured. As with all such cases, the main problem for anybody subsequently investigating such events is evidence. Unlike other similar massacres there were no survivors of what happened at Ardenne Abbey; the only way of ascertaining who was responsible was to carry out a detailed and thorough investigation. On this occasion that job fell to the officers and men of the Canadian War Crimes Commission under the command of Lieutenant Colonel Bruce Macdonald. The investigation took them the best part of a year to complete, but because they did such a thorough job, Meyer was subsequently found guilty at his subsequent war crimes trial. It has to be said, the final outcome was a bittersweet one.

Chapter Six

The Malmedy Massacres

On the first morning of the Battle of the Bulge, 16 December 1944, 1st Lieutenant Kyle Joseph Bouck Jr was in charge of eighteen men of the Intelligence and Reconnaissance Platoon, attached to the 394th Infantry Regiment, 99th United States Infantry Division, and four forward artillery observers from 'C' Battery, 371st Field Artillery.

Bouck and his men found themselves defending an important road junction in an area known as the Losheim Gap, which was the main route of advance for German armoured units, specifically Kampfgruppe SS Standartenführer Joachim Peiper's 1st SS Panzer Division, the spearhead unit of the 6th Panzer Army under the command of SS-Oberstgruppenführer Sepp Dietrich.

The job of clearing the road of American forces through this area fell to the men of the 1st Battalion, 9th Fallschirmjäger, or Parachute Regiment, who were part of the 3rd Fallschirmjäger Division. At 8am on 16 December, Peiper and his tanks were held up for most of the morning along the Blankenheim-Schnied road, which was heavily congested with a number of different men and vehicles. Some 500 German paratroopers had been held up for most of the day by Lieutenant Bouck and the twenty-two men under his command. Word finally reached Peiper at 6pm that evening that the paratroopers had managed to overcome the Americans at Lanzerath Ridge, taken them prisoner and secured the nearby village of Lanzerath, thus allowing the 600 vehicles of Joachim Peiper's 1st SS Panzer Division to advance.

The fight put up by Bouck and his men was a truly remarkable one, taking into account they were outnumbered some fifty to one. Without realising it, possibly because they were eventually overrun and captured, what they did that day in holding up the Germans, and killing and wounding ninety-two of their elite paratroopers, caused a major disruption to the advance in that sector of Dietrich's entire 6th Panzer Army. After finally being outflanked, Bouck and his remaining men were captured by the German paratroopers. They then spent a further two days marching in extremely inclement weather, before being loaded on to a train along with a number of other captured Americans at the village of Junkerath. It was far from being a comfortable journey, as they were crammed into a boxcar for days on end without food or water.

They even had to suffer the indignity of being attacked by their own aircraft on 21 December, an attack which saw a number of them killed and wounded.

Lieutenant Lyle Bouck Jr., deserves a mention because at the time he was only 20 years of age, and when called upon to do his bit, he did not falter. He faced the challenge and passed with flying colours. Bouck and his men were greatly outnumbered by their enemy, yet fought to hold them off for more than fifteen hours, with many of their number wounded. As it turns out, these men were incredibly fortunate to be captured and dealt with by German paratroopers rather than Peiper and his men, who were delayed further back down the road, because this saved them from the massacre that occurred at Malmedy the following day.

At the time, neither Bouck and his men nor the American military authorities fully appreciated the real significance of what had been achieved that day. Because of Bouck and his small band of very brave men, Dietrich's 6th Panzer Army got nowhere near achieving their target for the day of reaching the Meuse River, instead they had hardly gained any ground at all, greatly delaying the German attack, which in turn allowed the Americans to solidify their positions. If it hadn't been for the defensive action of 16 December 1944, the Battle of the Bulge would have more than likely turned very differently.

The sad thing about this, the actions of Bouck and his men were never truly recognised. Because they were captured, Bouck had not made and submitted a combat report and when he was finally released from captivity in May 1945, he was too ill to even think about belatedly doing so. Bouck didn't see what he and his men had done as being anything significant. As far as he was concerned, their capture was a failure. He and his men had been attacked and were simply doing their best to stay alive.

It was only in the years after the war, when books were being written about the Battle of the Bulge, that the significance of what they had done started to be appreciated. Even then it took a lot of letter-writing by Bouck and lobbying of politicians before the men of the Intelligence and Reconnaissance Platoon received their due recognition.

On 26 October 1981, nearly thirty-six years after the events had taken place, every member of Bouck's platoon was awarded the Presidential Unit Citation, they also received a total of nineteen medals for their valour, making them one of the most highly decorated platoons of the Second World War.

On 17 December, the day after Bouck's heroic actions, a convoy of some thirty American military vehicles, mainly from 'B' Battery, of the 285th Field Artillery Observation Battalion, arrived at the Baugnez crossroads near Malmedy, where they found themselves confronted by Peiper and his Kampfgruppe unit of armoured vehicles and half-tracks.

Their Panzer tanks opened fire destroying the lead American vehicles, bringing the convoy to an immediate halt and rendering the rest of the vehicles and men, 'sitting ducks'.

The American convoy was quickly overcome and its men captured and taken prisoner. They were placed in an adjacent field, and without any warning, Peiper's men opened fire on their unarmed and unsuspecting captives, killing eighty-four of them in the process.

Once captured and rounded up, one of the SS tank commanders ordered one of the SS privates to fire into the American prisoners. This was just the beginning as machine-gun fire from both the Panzer tanks and SS soldiers killed and wounded more and more of the Americans. When the firing had ceased, some of the SS soldiers walked among the dead and dying, asking in English if anybody needed medical assistance, those who replied were immediately shot dead. There was no consideration given to burying the dead Americans, in an attempt to hide what they had done. Instead Peiper and his men left their bodies where they had fallen, and simply moved on.

This was to be the worst massacre of American troops that took place in Europe throughout the Second World War. Fortunately for mankind and humanity as a whole, not all of the Americans had been killed. Once the Germans had left the area, the wounded men made good their escape, back to the safety of their own lines to tell their horrific story. It helped stiffen the resolve of American troops, who now saw no point in even thinking about surrendering to German forces, believing that to do so meant certain death. It no doubt also caused problems for German forces, who ran the risk of American forces hell bent on exacting revenge committing similar acts upon any of their combatants who might have considered surrendering.

The main objective of the Battle of the Bulge was the capture of Antwerp in Belgium, but to do this, the 6th SS Panzer Army, led by SS General Sepp Dietrich had to cross the River Meuse from the German side. For this action to succeed, the Germans needed to capture bridges in the Belgium town of Huy. The man tasked with making this happen was Obersturmbannführer Joachim Peiper. To achieve this would be no easy feat for three main reasons. First, a lack of readily available fuel. Remember, this was just five months from Germany's surrender to the Allies and the end of the Second World War, and the army was running low on fuel, men and equipment. Second, the roads that Peiper would have to travel along were not suitable for the heavily armoured Tiger II tanks attached to his Kampfgruppe. But the toughest element of

Peiper being able to achieve his task was the need for a rapid advance through American lines.

In the book *Malmedy Massacre*, Richard Gallagher writes that during the operational briefing, Peiper told his men that no quarter was to be shown to enemy combatants, no prisoners were to be taken; although not to be directly targeted, if Belgian civilians got in the way, then that was just unfortunate.

There is a forgotten irony attached to Peiper's advance. His favoured route to his first objective at the Belgian village of Losheimergraben wasn't possible. This was the exact same route taken in 1940 when the Germans had invaded Belgium and France, Field Marshal Erwin Rommel's division sped through the Losheim Gap to gain the Meuse River and then push on to the English Channel. Earlier in 1944, when the Germans had been forced to retreat along the same route, they had blown up the Losheim-Losheimergr road bridge, and it had not subsequently been repaired, so Peiper was unable to use that particular route. He eventually decided to travel through Lanzerath to Bucholz Station, but his progression was a lot slower than he had planned, mainly due to the road he had taken being clogged up with other German military vehicles.

Peiper's plan had been full of 'what ifs', which all needed to happen if his mission was to succeed. For example, the Belgium village of Lanzereth was still in American hands when he set out on his operation.

Survivor

One of the men who survived the massacre at Malmedy was William Merriken, who served with the 285th Field Artillery Observation Battalion.

Local resident Emile Jamar played a key role in saving Merriken and his colleague Charles E. Reding in the immediate aftermath of the massacre. In an interview in April 1999, Jamar explained how Merriken and Reding were reunited with their battalion.

Mrs Anna Blaise-Cerexhe, a widow, took in the two wounded American soldiers on the afternoon of 17 December 1944. Despite her best efforts, the health of the two men deteriorated and Anna knew their best hope of survival was to get them back to their battalion in Malmedy a couple of miles away. Unfortunately, Anna could speak no English and the soldiers couldn't speak French, so communication was difficult. Reding wrote a message and gave it to Anna, who took it to her neighbours the Jamars.

One of the Jamars' seven children was 15-year-old Emile. He was the local paperboy and not only knew his way around, but knew all the shortcuts to take, not just locally, but from village to village between his home and Malmedy.

Because of his paper round, he was well known, so his presence would not draw any undue attention.

Emile said he would deliver Reding's message by hiding it in his shoe. If he was stopped and searched by a German soldier, the chances were he would not be asked to remove his shoes. It was still a dangerous and brave thing to do; if he was found with the note on him, he would undoubtedly have been tortured until he divulged where the Americans were being hidden. Not only would the soldiers have been shot, but also the entire Jamar family, along with Madame Blaise-Cerexhe.

Despite all these concerns, Emile set off for Malmedy with the nervous blessing of his parents. Time was of the essence, not only for the Americans, but for the Jamars and Madame Blaise-Cerexhe; the longer the soldiers were in their midst, the more chance there was of being discovered.

By the time Emile set off for Malmedy it was already ten o'clock in the morning. As if his journey wasn't dangerous enough, as he neared his destination he came across a number of metallic plates scattered across the road. Although he had heard about mines, he didn't really understand what they were and, possibly because of his age, did not fully appreciate just how dangerous and life-threatening they were. Fortunately for Emile it was daytime and he was able to walk, quickly but carefully, through the mines without stepping on any of them, a feat which would no doubt have cost him his life if he had taken the same journey during the hours of darkness.

Not that much further down the road beyond the 'minefield' at the end of Mon Bijou Avenue, where he had to cross over the railway line, he came upon a roadblock. It was a nervous moment for the young Emile, as he didn't know whether it was American or German. He didn't have to wait long to find out; two American soldiers suddenly appeared from where they had been hiding, rifles at the ready, both of which were pointing directly towards a startled Emile. Once again there was a language barrier to overcome, but to no avail. The two American soldiers, maybe uncertain of what to do with their new-found Belgian friend, escorted him to the other end of the Avenue, by the Café Loffet, where they placed him in the back of a jeep and drove him to the local primary school at Francorchamps.

Still they could not find any American soldier who could speak French. Back in the jeep, they set off again, this time to a hotel in Hockay, about thirty miles and an hour's drive away.

At Hockay they finally found an American captain who could speak French. Emile explained the situation, removed his shoe and handed over the note from Charles Reding. American soldiers were suddenly rushing all over the place as they prepared to go with Emile back to Madame Blaise-Cerexhe's home. Before they left Emile remembered that his mother had asked him to see if he could acquire some bread from the Americans. Emile asked, and as if by magic he was quickly handed three fresh white loaves of bread by a happy and grateful American soldier. Before long Emile was in the back of an American lorry along with several soldiers on their way back to Malmedy.

At Malmedy there was an ambulance waiting for them. Emile changed vehicles and sat in the rear of the ambulance so he could speak to the driver through a sliding hatch separating him from the driver's cab, allowing him to provide directions to the driver on how to get to their wounded comrades. They made their way through a couple of roadblocks and reached the place where the mines are scattered across the road. They turned out to be American, laid there to provide an early warning of any Germans that might be making their way towards their position at Malmedy.

It took more than an hour to remove enough mines to allow the ambulance and army truck through, with a dozen soldiers in it, guns at the ready, so they could get to the wounded men as quickly and safely as possible. Once through that last obstacle, it did not take them long to get to their comrades. Having arrived at Chapelle de Geromont, Emile directed the driver of the ambulance up a dirt track towards Madame Blaise-Cerexhe's farm, and to the barn where the two wounded Americans were hiding. Understandably, Anna was very happy to see them. In no time at all the American medics were treating their wounded comrades, who were relieved and happy to know they were finally safe from being discovered.

After a quick examination, the two soldiers exchanged thankful smiles with Madam Blaise-Cerexhe, their guardian angel, without whose bravery they would have likely not survived. Placed on stretchers, they were lifted into the back of the ambulance, but not before Anna leant over and gave one of them a gentle kiss. It was a tearful goodbye. The rear doors of the ambulance closed and as fast as safely possible, it made the short journey back to Malmedy so that William Merriken and Charles Reding could receive the medical attention they so urgently required.

It had been a long, tiring, yet exciting day for young Emile, and one that could have ended so badly for him and his family if he had been stopped by the Germans. As it was, the two American soldiers were saved and Emile had managed to acquire three loaves of hard-to-come-by bread for his mother. Both Emile and Madame Blaise-Cerexhe went on to survive the war; Emile died on 6 October 2006 and Madame Blaise-Cerexhe passed away in 1971. There is one final piece to write about in relation to the Malmedy massacre and that is another war crime that was committed during the Battle of the Bulge, for which it could be argued that Joachim Peiper was also responsible.

On 1 January 1945, near Chenogne, Belgium, eighty members of the Führerbegleitbrigade, a German armoured brigade and the 3rd Panzergrenadier Division, were lined up in a field and machine-gunned by American soldiers from the United States 11th Armoured Division, just two weeks after the massacre at Malmedy, an event which caused much outrage among American forces, especially those involved in the fighting of the Battle of the Bulge.

Staff Sergeant John W. Fague, 'B' Company, 21st Armoured Infantry Battalion, part of the United States 11th Armoured Division, gave the following description of the massacre at Chenogne:

> Some of the boys had some prisoners line up. I knew they were going to shoot them, and I hated this business …. They marched the prisoners back up the hill to murder them with the rest of the prisoners we had secured that morning …. As we were going up the hill out of town, I know some of our boys were lining up German prisoners in the fields on both sides of the road. There must have been 25 to 30 German boys in each group. Machine guns were being set up. These boys were to be machine gunned and murdered. We were committing the same crimes we were now accusing the Japs and Germans of doing …. Going back down the road into town I looked in to the fields where the German boys had been shot. Dark lifeless forms lay in the snow.

Another American soldier, Max Cohen, also witnessed the same massacre as described by Fague. Referring to the massacre at Chenogne, General George S. Patton made an entry in his diary for 4 January 1945: 'Also murdered 50 odd German men. I hope we can cover it up'.

No one was ever prosecuted for their part in the murders of the German soldiers at Chenogne, and the name of the commanding officer of 'B' Company, 21st Armoured Infantry Battalion, 11th Armoured Division, although recorded in a file or archive somewhere, is not commonly known.

Maybe what took place at Chenogne was directly linked to the actions of Peiper and his men at Malmedy, maybe it was an act of revenge by American soldiers for the murder of their comrades. Maybe it was because, having lost many of their own men at Chenogne, they simply wanted revenge for their deaths. Either way, it was wrong. It is strange that so much is known about Malmedy, but Chenogne is rarely mentioned in the history of the Second

World War and the Battle of the Bulge, although both events related to the mass murder of unarmed enemy prisoners of war.

While researching this book I was interested to discover that while it was relatively straightforward to find the names of the American soldiers murdered by German forces at Wereth and Malmedy, I was unable to find a list of the German soldiers murdered by American forces at Chenogne. This, I believe, is a good example of how history becomes blurred, because it tends to be written by the victors and is usually one-sided. While the victors' account highlights its own famous victories, along with the inadequacies of vanquished nations, it also fails to admit, or attempts to justify, or simply covers up its own failings. The committing of a wrong by one side cannot justify the committing of a similar act by the other. It is simply an act of revenge.

It is clear that during the Battle of the Bulge there were numerous massacres carried out by both sides, but history only appears to have highlighted those carried out by German forces in an attempt to demonise them, while at the same time justifying or ignoring the actions of American forces.

Chapter Seven

The Wereth Massacre

Although much has been written about the Malmedy massacre of 17 December 1944, history has told us less about the eleven American soldiers murdered earlier that same day at the nearby Belgian village of Wereth. Although there was not a cover up of the murders, the incident does not appear to have been investigated as rigorously as the Malmedy massacre. Why, I will leave you to decide.

The families of the men were not informed about the specifics of how their loved ones were killed, instead, they simply received official letters from the American War Office, informing them that they had been killed in action while fighting for their country.

The eleven men, all Black American soldiers, who were serving with the United States Army's 333rd Field Artillery Battalion, were killed by SS troops of the 1st SS Panzer Division, LSSAH, after they had laid down their arms and surrendered.

The 333rd Field Artillery Regiment was formed, using the language of the time, as a 'coloured or segregated' unit at Camp Gruber, Oklahoma, and became part of the United States 3rd Army. They first arrived in Europe after landing by sea at Normandy in July 1944. Three months later in October, they found themselves in the small Belgium village of Schoenberg. The unit's four Batteries were split with one of them being situated on the west side of the Our River, with the other three located on the east side. All four of the Batteries were equipped with the M1114 155mm howitzer artillery guns.

On the morning of 16 December 1940, Adolf Hitler unleashed his surprise Wacht am Rhein plan, with the objective being to retake the Belgium city port of Antwerp. It was also referred to as the Ardennes Offensive, or the von Rundstedt Offensive, after the German Generalfeldmarschall Gerd von Rundstedt, although somewhat ironically it was not a plan he was entirely supportive of as he believed it was somewhat ambitious, an opinion which ultimately proved to be correct. It took place in an area that covers parts of eastern Belgium, north east France and Switzerland; the last major German offensive of the Second World War, it was referred to by the Allies as the Battle of the Bulge.

For this surprise attack Germany deployed troops of the Waffen SS, under the command of Major Gustav Knittel, who were ordered to unleash a wave of terror that did not allow for any feelings of humanity towards their enemies. Why such behaviour was demanded of them is unclear, as it certainly wasn't in keeping with the rules of war laid down by the terms of the Geneva Convention.

The village of Schoenberg and its surrounding areas came under a heavy German artillery bombardment in the early hours of 16 December 1944. Two of the Batteries, A and B, moved further West, while C and the Service Battalion remained to offer support for the 14th Cavalry Regiment. The following morning Schoenberg was captured by rapidly advancing German forces. The Service Battery of the 333rd Field Artillery Regiment, having left it as late as they could, tried to make good their escape to the neighbouring village of St Vith via a bridge which separated the two locations, but it was too late as the bridge was already in German hands. The Americans came under attack which resulted in a number of their men being killed or wounded. They were quickly overcome and those still alive were captured and taken prisoner by the Germans. Soon after this, the German column, with its newly acquired prisoners of war, came under attack by an American aircraft.

Understandably in such circumstances, confusion and self-preservation rapidly ensued and eleven of the prisoners took the opportunity to make good their escape. The same afternoon they reached the small hamlet of Wereth, which consisted of just nine homes.

Before the First World War Wereth hadn't been in Belgium, rather it had been part of Germany; twenty years later, at the beginning of the Second World War, it was still a divided village with three of the families still seeing themselves as German rather than Belgian. The fleeing Americans, of course, had no way of knowing this. But luck was on their side. Having been on the run for more than six hours, wet through as a result of it having rained for most of the day and with darkness fast falling, they approached the first of the houses, which was owned by Mathias and Maria Langer, who, fortunately, were not one of the families with German sympathies. The Langers invited the Americans into their home, offering them shelter and food. This was an extremely brave thing to do, because if the Germans had found out, it could have resulted in not only their deaths, but their children's as well.

It wouldn't be too long before the Americans' presence in Wereth became known by the residents of the entire hamlet. One of them was the wife of a serving German soldier and it is believed this woman informed German forces who were out looking for the escaped American prisoners that they were hiding in one of the homes. The SS soldiers quickly discovered the men, who surrendered quietly.

The eleven Americans were told to sit down at the back of the house by the SS troops, which they willingly did, having absolutely no idea of the fate that was about to befall them. Once the SS troops had gathered their thoughts, they marched them off to a nearby field where they killed them. Their deaths were both brutal and prolonged. For them there was no expediency of a machine gun burst across the chest or a bullet to the back of the head, instead they were stabbed, beaten and tortured before they died.

Six weeks later the village and the surrounding area was recaptured by American forces from the 99th Division, who discovered the bodies of their murdered comrades still laying in the field where they were killed. Their frozen bodies, preserved by the winter snows, did not make for a pretty sight. Major James L. Baldwin of the 99th Division, who was the first American to see the bodies of his dead comrades, took photographs and documented in a written report what he had witnessed. Their faces had been battered, their legs broken, some had fingers cut off while others had been stabbed with bayonets. Why the SS troops felt the need to brutalise and mutilate the American soldiers in such a manner was never explained in subsequent war crimes trials, and all these years later, it still makes absolutely no sense at all.

Major Baldwin's report was so sensitive, it was almost immediately deemed to be classified and forwarded to the War Crimes Commission. But inexplicably, it was closed in 1948 without any further investigation or action having been carried out.

By the time that the Battle of the Bulge was over, the 333rd Field Artillery Battalion had sustained more losses than any other artillery unit in the United States Army 8th Corps. A total of six officers and 222 listed men had either been killed or captured.

Thankfully, Mathias and Maria Langer and their two children, Tina and Herman, were not punished by the SS for their act of kindness towards the American soldiers.

Although it cannot be proved beyond all reasonable doubt which individuals were responsible for the murders, it is known that they were members of the 1st Panzer Division SS LSSAH. It is worth pointing out that the distance between Wereth and Malmedy is only about fifteen miles, a journey which in a vehicle would take no longer than about twenty-five minutes to complete, meaning it would have been more than possible for Joachim Peiper and his men to have carried out both atrocities.

The Langers' son Herman was only 12 years of age when the American soldiers stayed, albeit briefly, at their home. It was something he never forgot. In 1990, he placed a simple wooden cross on the spot where the American soldiers were murdered. In May 2004, a memorial to the eleven men was unveiled in the same field.

In 1949, the United States Senate Armed Services Committee investigated a dozen incidents of unarmed American prisoners of war who had been murdered in Belgium during the period of the Battle of the Bulge, but the Committee's final report inexcusably made no mention whatsoever, of the murder of the eleven black American soldiers who had been brutally murdered at Wereth.

Sadly, little has been written about the massacre, and it is certainly not a story known by the wider American population. Rob Wilkins, a member of the World History Group and a retired master sergeant in the United States Air Force, came across the story while researching Black Americans who had served in the US military during the course of the Second World War. He in turn took the story to the American newspaper, *USA Today*; one of its reporters, Jim Michaels, wrote an article entitled 'Massacre of 11 Black Soldiers', which appeared in the paper's edition of 8 November 2013, some seventy-three years after the event had taken place.

In the 1st Session of the 116th Congress of the United States of America, which took place on 12 December 2019, a resolution was passed under the heading: 'Honoring the 75th Anniversary of the Battle of the Bulge, fought during World War ll; Congressional Record volume 165, No. 199.'

The resolution officially recognised the valiant efforts made by American forces, along with those of other Allied nations in December 1944, especially those who were killed. Their collective efforts contributed to an Allied victory in the European Theatre of war. In relation to the Wereth II, the resolution stated:

> Whereas 11 African American soldiers of the 333rd Field Artillery Battalion were massacred by SS Troops near Wereth, Belgium, and were identified as:
>
> Private (Medic) 34511454 Curtis Adams, of South Carolina.
>
> Corporal 34046336 Mager Bradley, of Bolivar County, Mississippi.
>
> Private 1st Class 34553436 George Davis, Junior, of Jefferson County, Alabama.
>
> Staff Sergeant 34046992 Thomas J. Forte, of Jackson, Mississippi.

Technician 5th Grade 34552457 Robert Leroy Green, Upson County, Georgia.

Private 1st Class 34481753 James L. Leatherwood, of Pontotoc, Mississippi.

Private 38040062 Nathaniel Moss, of Longview, Texas.

Private 1st Class 38304695 George Moten, of Hopkins County, Texas.

Technician 4th Grade 34552760 William Edward Pritchett, of Camden, Alabama.

Technician 4th Grade 35744547 James A Stewart, of Piedmont, West Virginia.

Private 1st Class 383833 Due W. Turner, of Arkansas.

It is staggering that it took seventy-nine years for there to be any official recognition of the appalling circumstance surrounding the deaths of these brave young men by the country for which they fought and died.

Seven of the men were buried at the American Cemetery of Henri-Chapelle, which is located some 30 kilometres from the Belgian city of Liege. The remains of the other four men were returned to the United States.

Each of the men was posthumously awarded a Purple Heart for their service and sacrifice to their country.

Chapter Eight

Malmedy Massacre: Arrest, Trial and Conviction

The war had been unravelling for some time as far as Germany was concerned and by the beginning of 1945, it had become clear to all concerned that it was a matter of 'when' she would be defeated rather than 'if'. The Ardennes Offensive had failed, and Hitler's last realistic attempt at saving the war was Operation Spring Awakening. The aim was to prevent Soviet forces from advancing on Vienna in Austria, while trying to secure important oil reserves located to the south of Lake Balaton in Hungary. But after ten days of fighting the operation stalled and, in essence, that was the end of the war for Germany, although she managed to hold out for nearly two more months, fighting Soviet forces in the east and Allied forces to the south and west.

As best we know, Hitler committed suicide in his bunker in Berlin on 30 April 1945, a fact Peiper and his men were informed of the following day while they were in Austria. A week later, on 8 May, Peiper received orders to cross the Enns River, a tributary of the great River Danube, and surrender to American forces which, however precarious, was a much better option than being captured by the Soviets. Peiper didn't fancy either option and decided to make his way home. Before he was able to do that, however, he was arrested by American forces on 22 May 1945, although at that stage they were unaware of his true identity, and as far as they were concerned he was just another German prisoner of war for them to look after and feed.

In the early stages of his incarceration, Peiper was held in a prisoner of war camp in Bavaria, Germany, along with hundreds of other prisoners, both ordinary German soldiers and SS men alike. But it quickly became apparent to the American intelligence officers and the commandant of the camp that Peiper was no ordinary prisoner and that others looked up to him. He openly and calmly derided the Jews and Poles when questioned on the topic by his American captors, without any apparent fear or concern for the words that he said.

What Peiper would not have known was that an investigation by the Americans was already underway concerning the Malmedy massacre, and that they knew this and other similar crimes had been committed by Kampfgruppe

Peiper. The job of finding surviving members of the unit had not been an easy task because at the time there were some 4 million German prisoners of war in Allied captivity. As for Peiper, his luck ran out on 21 August 1945 when, after having been transferred to another camp, his name came to the attention of the camp's commandant. At last the Americans had their number one target, and he was sent to a military intelligence interrogation centre in the Bavarian town of Freising.

At the height of their investigation the Americans had identified 1,000 former SS men who had served in the LSSAH unit, all of whom were moved from a number of different camps all over Germany to a prison in the town of Schwäbisch Hall. Peiper arrived there in December 1945, where he remained until April 1946, when he was once again moved, this time to Dachau concentration camp, where he was put on trial for war crimes.

The main problem with the prosecution and conviction of those responsible for ordering or carrying out war-time massacres of captured enemy troops, or civilians of occupied territories, is that there were rarely any surviving witnesses to the events. Sometimes it is down to guesswork or supposition, based on nothing more damming than records showing that a particular military unit, or units, were in a particular area at a given time when it is known a massacre took place.

As adjutant to Himmler, not only would it be ridiculous to suggest that Peiper would have had no knowledge of the Holocaust, but that he also had no involvement in the policy-making process of its implementation. This would have been the same in relation to the wartime ethnic cleansing and widespread murder carried out by the SS and Nazi Germany throughout Europe.

It was very rare for an individual who was subsequently arrested and charged with having committed a war crime, to make a full and frank admission about what they were alleged to have done; such an admission would more than likely have guaranteed their own death.

Where there were survivors or witnesses to such an atrocity, one of the main problems often faced by prosecutors was identification of the suspect, or suspects, and confirmation that they had actually been there at the time. This was particularly the case when a commanding officer was the person who had ordered his men to carry out a massacre, but was not present himself when it was carried out.

In Peiper's case things were totally different. When he stood trial, despite facing allegations and accusations that he had been responsible for the murder of Allied prisoners of war and innocent civilians, and had more than likely witnessed other war crimes, he did not actually deny anything. He even went as far as to take full responsibility for his own actions as well as those of the men under his command.

When asked about these matters in the years after the war, he often resorted to saying he could not recollect the exact details of what he had done. He was actually called upon to be a prosecution witness against some of his former colleagues in a number of post-war trials. On each occasion he claimed that he had the failing memory of an old man and because of this he could not recollect specific details of what he was being asked about.

The following article appeared in the *Bradford Observer* newspaper dated Monday 1 January 1945.

> **Helpless Men Raked with Fire**
> **Americans Describe Malmedy Massacre**
> Results of the preliminary investigation by the American authorities into the shooting by the Germans of some 115 American prisoners near Malmedy, at the opening of Von Rundstedts' recent counter-offensive, were released at SHAEF last night.
>
> The massacred men were mostly from a field artillery observation battalion, and their story is told by 15 who escaped.
>
> Their battery was travelling in convoy on 17 December, and arrived at the junction of the highways of St Vith and Waimes when a number of German tanks travelling in the opposite direction were observed.
>
> The Germans opened fire immediately and the Americans abandoned their vehicles to seek cover. Shortly, however, the whole battery's personnel were captured and rounded up in an open field.
>
> After taking away their cigarettes and valuables the German guard suddenly fired in to the defenceless group.
>
> Shortly afterwards two German tanks began spraying the Americans with machine-gun fire from between 75 and 120 feet. Dead and wounded prisoners fell to the ground as did those who were not hit.
>
> The American authorities believe that those who were not hit at first were later killed when the German gunners continued spraying them on the ground.
>
> When the tanks left the field, German infantrymen on top of them fired small arms into the helpless mass as a parting gesture. Finally, German soldiers walked through the mass of bodies deliberately shooting men still showing signs of life.

> Between 20 and 25 Americans, who, even after this were only wounded, decided to make a run for it. The German guards opened up at them again, but 15 managed to escape.

The Birmingham Daily Gazette newspaper dated Monday 20 August 1945, included a brief article about Joachim Peiper's arrest and detention:

> **US Troops Find Their Man**
> **'No.1 War Criminal' was in PoW Cage**
> An eight month search for the man responsible for the mass slaughter of more than 100 American infantry prisoners near Malmedy during the Battle of the Bulge last December, has ended.
>
> The criminal Colonel Joachim Peipper, aged 30, a former adjutant to Himmler, was found hiding among 10,000 SS troops in a prison cage.
>
> His connection with the Malmedy massacre was revealed after hours of questioning.
>
> Major Clisson, commandant of the SS prisoners' of war camp, said that Peiper was the US troops Public Enemy No.1.

Major Clisson was the commandant of Landsberg Prison in Bavaria, Germany, where all convicted SS officers and soldiers were held after their trials. Between 1945 and 1946, a total of 1,544 Germans convicted of war crimes were held at the prison. Of these a total of 288 were executed, 259 of which were hanged and a further twenty-nine were shot by firing squad.

The *Sunderland Daily Echo and Shipping Gazette* dated Thursday 31 January 1946, included the following story on its back page about that day's events at the Nuremberg trials. One of the stories was about the Malmedy massacre.

> A documented account of the massacre of 129 unarmed US soldiers near Malmedy during the German Ardennes Offensive in December 1944, was presented.
>
> While M. Dubost (Prosecutor) was describing the massacre, Goering hung his head, states Chas Lynch (Reuter).
>
> A Nazi officer indulged in target practice on the 129 Americans as a prelude to their cold blooded murder. A statement by a German soldier described the massacre at a crossroads.
>
> The Americans were led to a field, where the Nazis searched each man, taking watches, rings and other effects. A German armoured

vehicle was then manoeuvred so that its guns were trained on the Americans.

A German officer dismounted from the vehicle, took a revolver, aimed and fired. One of the prisoners fell. The officer then aimed again, and another man fell. As the second man dropped, machine gun fire was opened up from the vehicle on the little group of prisoners, spraying lead for two or three minutes, killing most of them and injuring the others.

Later German soldiers walked among the group, and those Americans who were still alive were finished off.

'The shame of this deed will remain upon the German Army', the German soldier's statement went on. 'We knew that these men were unarmed and had surrendered.'

The German soldier who made the statement was not named in the article, neither was the German officer who used some of the prisoners for target practice, but it is quite possible that this man was Joachim Peiper.

The *Hartlepool Northern Daily Mail* newspaper dated Tuesday 21 May 1946, carried the following headline story on its front page:

Nazis laughed as they shot us

German soldiers laughed as they attacked unarmed American prisoners of war with machine-guns and revolvers in a field near Malmedy, Belgium, during the German Ardennes push at Christmas 1944, Virgil Lary, a former US lieutenant, told the Dachau war crimes court today, reports Reuter.

Three German generals and 71 soldiers were before the court charged with the massacre of US prisoners of war.

Lary said: 'I fell to the ground with my face in the mud. Men fell dead and wounded all round me. The firing lasted about three minutes. Then I heard agonising screams from a wounded man. There was a single pistol shot and the screams ceased.

I heard German laughter and later more machine-gun fire, more pistol shots, and more laughter.'

Lary pointed out George Fleps, a Rumanian SS private, as the man who fired a pistol in to a group of some hundred prisoners.

At the end of the Second World War, the Judge Advocate's Department of the Third US Army set up a branch of its own to investigate and prosecute

German military personnel who had been identified as having committed war crimes against American soldiers. Between 1945 and 1948 it oversaw a total of 489 court proceedings which involved war crimes charges against a total of 1,672 German officers and soldiers.

Over the years there has been a certain amount of controversy about some of these cases, which asked the question whether what happened was justice or revenge. One of, if not the, most controversial of these cases was the one involving those charged with the murder of American prisoners of war at Malmedy.

Fleps would have undoubtedly escaped punishment for his crimes if Lary had not survived the massacre to bear witness.

Without wishing to cast any doubt on Lary's version of the events of that day, I have to ask the obvious question. If, at his own admission, he was lying face down in the mud almost immediately the shooting began, how was it possible for him to clearly identify Fleps, who no doubt would have been wearing a helmet or some other type of head gear.

A surprise witness also provided evidence on Peiper's behalf. None other than a United States Army Lieutenant Colonel Hal McCown, who was the commanding officer of the 2nd Battalion, 119th Infantry Regiment, 30th Infantry Division, and had been a prisoner of Peiper's battle group.

McCown and his men were captured at La Gleize on 21 December 1944, just four days after the massacres at Wereth, Malmedy and other nearby villages, by soldiers from Peiper's unit. With Peiper in effect surrounded at La Gleize, he and McCown negotiated over American prisoners of war, who were eventually released when Peiper and his men fled on foot and headed towards German lines, having destroyed their vehicles before they left.

The picture that had been painted about Peiper being a bloodthirsty, cold-blooded murderer was not a description that McCown readily recognised. In a report he submitted to his superiors after he and his men had been released, this is what he had to say:

> Concerning treatment of prisoners by the SS, I can state that at no time were the prisoners of this organization mistreated. Food was scarce but it was nearly as good as that used by the Germans themselves. The American prisoners were always given cellar space to protect them from the exceedingly heavy American artillery barrages. I was taken for a brief period to the main prisoner enclosure which was a large two-room, well-constructed cellar quite superior to any I saw in La Gleize. The men were considerably overcrowded and were allowing the guards to bully them a little. I organized the

entire group of some 130 into sections, appointed a First Sergeant and laid down a few rules and got the German warrant officer in charge of the prisoners settled upon a fairer method of giving.

McCown remained in the army after the war and went on to serve during both the Korean war in 1951, and in Vietnam during 1962 and 1963.

An article appeared on the front page of the *Northern Whig* newspaper dated Wednesday 17 July 1946.

Bulge killers ask to be shot

Forty-three veterans of the German SS, including Colonel Joachim Peiper, were sentenced to death by an American military court at Dachau yesterday, for the slaughter of 900 American soldiers and Belgian civilians during the 'Battle of the Bulge'. Among those given life terms was General Joseph (Sepp) Dietrich, veteran of Adolf Hitler's 1923 beer hall putch in Munich.

Although the formal death sentence called for hanging, the men asked to be shot instead, and the court announced that the recommendation would be made to General McNarey, commanding general of American Forces in Europe. Women wept as the sentences were read in a courtroom jammed with people, about three-quarters of whom were German civilians.

The *Belfast News-Letter* dated Saturday 19 October 1946 had an article about Nazi war criminals who had been convicted and executed for their crimes. It does not include anything about Joachim Peiper, but it does include the Malmedy massacre.

The Hanged Nazis died like brave men, says executioner

Master-Sergeant John C. Woods who executed the 10 Nazis, has written an exclusive story for the Associated Press. He says:

I did a good job. I'll say this for those Nazis, they died like brave men. Only one of them showed any signs of weakening. When Frick was climbing those 13 steps of the gallows one leg seemed to go bad on him, and the guards had to steady him.

They were all arrogant. You could see they hated us. Old Jew baiter Streicher looked right at me when he said: 'The Bolsheviks will hang you too, some day'. And I looked him back in the eye. They can't bother me.'

After I started hanging these German war criminals last year, somebody tried to poison me here in Germany, and somebody shot at me in Paris, but the poison only made me sick and the bullet missed me.

The way I look at this hanging job, somebody has to do it. I got into it kind of by accident years ago in the States. I attended a hanging as a witness, and the hangman asked me if I'd mind helping. I did, and later I took over myself.

I may come back to Germany. There are more than 120 war criminals waiting to be hanged, including those 43 sentenced for the Malmedy massacre. I had some buddies killed in that massacre, and I'll come back here just to get even for them.

The *Bradford Observer* of Tuesday 6 September 1949 included a very interesting article concerning Malmedy:

Mock trials caused Nazi SS troops to confess

Four Americans who helped to convict 73 SS troopers of the Malmedy massacre, admitted yesterday that they used mock trials and tried to 'scare' confessions out of suspects. Butthey denied brutality.

They were testifying before a three-man sub-committee of the United States Senate which is investigating the convicts' charges of maltreatment. The lives of six men may hinge on the outcome.

The six are still under a death sentence for their roles in the slaughter of some 700 American prisoners of war near Malmedy, Belgium, during the Battle of the Bulge.

Bruno Jacob (New Jersey), an interpreter, was the only one of the four Americans who admitted he had even heard of any maltreatment. Jacob also admitted that suspects who refused to make confessions were sometimes put in a so-called death cell to scare confessions out of them.

All admitted the use of mock trials with fake judges presiding over benches decorated with candles and crucifix.

Harry Thon (New York), former war crimes interpreter, said the mock trials were not very effective in producing confessions. He said it took four weeks of questioning before any of the 600 suspects would admit any shooting of unarmed prisoners.

In the mock trials, the witnesses related, one investigator would play the role of prosecutor and another would pretend to be counsel

> for the defence. The defence counsel was supposed to win the suspect's confidence and get him to talk.
>
> They denied that they pronounced death sentences on people who refused to confess and that they pretended to be starting the executions.

Maybe this is the reason, or part of the reason, why some of the SS troopers who were initially sentenced to death had their sentences reviewed and reduced to terms of imprisonment.

The investigation by the sub-committee of the United States Senate took some seventeen months before it delivered its findings, during which time the SS troopers remained on death row. The stress that they were under during this time would have been immense.

The *Shields Evening* news dated Wednesday 31 January 1951 contained the following article about the 6 SS troopers and their colleagues who had also initially been condemned to death:

> **Condemned War Criminals Reprieved**
> American authorities today freed Alfred von Krupp, last owner of the giant arms firm, from prison and restored his property. At the same time, 21 of 28 war criminals under sentence of death were reprieved.
>
> The original confiscation order made against Krupp, by the Nuremberg War Crimes Tribunal, which in 1948 sentenced him to 12 years imprisonment, was revoked, and he is to be freed at once.
>
> **Six SS Troopers**
> Those who were spared from the gallows included six SS troopers convicted of murdering US soldiers in the infamous 'Malmedy massacre'.
>
> The reprieved men are in Lansberg prison, Bavaria, where they have spent several years not knowing whether they would be executed. Their death sentences were commuted to prison terms by US High Commissioner, John McCloy, and US Military Commander, General Handy.

Why and how the two men came to their conclusions was not explained, which was strange given they had been found guilty of murdering unarmed American prisoners of war. The relatives and families of the murdered men deserved an explanation as to why a number of those found responsible for the deaths of their loved ones had been reprieved just six years after the atrocities had been committed.

> At the same time, the US authorities modified many other prison terms which had been passed by American War Crimes Tribunals.
>
> With today's actions, the US authorities cleaned up all their outstanding war crimes cases, which have been perhaps the sorest point in German-Allied relations.
>
> The British announced recently that similar reviews will be made of 240 war crimes cases tried by their courts.
>
> Today's rulings do not affect the cases of the seven top Nazis, including former Deputy Führer, Rudolf Hess, who were convicted by the International War Crimes Tribunal in Nuremberg.

I believe it is clear from this article that there was a collective Allied reasoning behind the decisions to provide clemency to so many convicted German war criminals, although I have been unable to establish exactly what that reason was. If I had to take a guess, I would suggest it had something to do with the US and British authorities wanting the fledgling German government, led by Chancellor Konrad Adenauer, 'on board' against the growing threat of Soviet Communism, that had already begun sweeping across the post war countries of eastern Europe.

The *Belfast Telegraph* newspaper dated Wednesday 31 January 1951 included the following article:

> **21 Nazis Escape Gallows**
> **Reprieved after reviews of death sentences**
> **Seven are told they must hang**
>
> Twenty-one German war criminals were spared from the gallows today, including six SS troopers convicted of murdering US soldiers in the infamous 'Malmedy massacre' in which 142 unarmed US prisoners of war were machine-gunned in 1944.
>
> Their death sentences were commuted to prison terms by the US High Commissioner, Mr John McCloy, and the US Military Commander, General Handy.
>
> Seven death sentences were confirmed, including those on Oswald Pohl, former SS Major-General, head of Hitler's concentration camp system, and on Otto Ohlendorf, former SS General, who headed the

> execution squads which followed up the conquering German armies to wipe out civilian 'undesirables'.

The mention of the 'execution squads' is a reference to the Einsatzgruppe, as in 1941 Ohlendorf was appointed the commander of Einsatzgruppe D, who were responsible for the murders of large numbers of civilians in Moldova, Ukraine, the Crimea and the North Caucasus. He had become a member of the SS in 1936, as an 'economic consultant' and was also a committed and loyal Nazi. At his trial he showed no remorse for his war-time actions, believing he had done nothing wrong, showing more concern for the stress on his men for having to carry out the murders, rather than those who were murdered.

> At the same time, the US authorities modified many other prison terms which had been passed by American war crimes tribunals, reductions of from five to ten years made. The men reprieved have been confined to Landsberg Prison under death sentence for more than five years.
>
> General Handy announcing commutation of the six Malmedy death sentences to life imprisonment said: 'This does not mean that there is any doubt whatsoever that each was guilty of the offences charged.'
>
> The offences were associated with 'a confused, fluid and desperate combat action, a last attempt to turn the tide of Allied successes. The crimes are definitely distinguishable from the more deliberate killings in concentration camps. Moreover, these prisoners were of comparatively lower rank and were neither shown to be the ones who initiated nor advocated the idea of creating a wave of frightfulness.'

General Handy appears to have been somewhat confused. How he could say, when talking about the six members of the SS who had been convicted for their part in carrying out the Malmedy massacre, that they had not been responsible for deliberate killings, beggars belief. With one of the six being Joachim Peiper, a lieutenant colonel in the SS, how could he possibly be classed as being of a 'comparatively lower rank'?

The most startling bit of the article has been saved for the end:

> All the SS troopers remaining under the death sentence for the 'Malmedy massacre' were saved from the gallows by General Handy's ruling. This means that no German will be executed for one of the worst atrocities of the war.

> Several hundred captured, unarmed US soldiers and Belgian civilians were shot down in cold blood by SS troops in and near Malmedy, Belgium, during the Battle of the Bulge.
>
> Seventy-four SS men were tried by a US military court in 1946 on charges of participating in these shootings. Seventy-three were convicted and 43 sentenced to hang, but subsequent reviews brought commutation of the death sentences to all but six.

The more I read this article, the more I am shocked at how General Handy came to the conclusions he did. It is almost as though there was an ulterior motive behind his decision, maybe a politically motivated one. Another question this also throws up is, why had these men not had their sentences carried out by 1951?

The *Northern Whig* newspaper of Monday 16 April 1956 includes an article about Joachim Peiper, and the attempts of some of his ex-comrades to have him released.

> **Germans ask for release of 'GIs' Enemy No.1'**
>
> Former Nazi SS soldiers have begun a campaign for the release of one of their leaders, Lieutenant-Colonel Joachim Peiper, now serving a life sentence in Landsberg Prison, Bavaria, for his part in the 'Malmedy' massacre of American prisoners-of-war in 1944. Peiper was once known as the 'GIs' Enemy No.1'.
>
> His unit was blamed for the shooting of 71 Americans at a crossroads south-east of Malmedy in Belgium. Peiper with other men in his unit, was sentenced to death by an American court, but the sentences were not carried out because US Army inquiries established that there had been irregularities in the original investigation of the crime.
>
> Peiper is one of three men still held in Landsberg for the Malmedy crime. The cases of all three are before the mixed German-Allied Clemency board who can recommend premature release of men sentenced for war crimes.

This demonstrates the level of esteem in which Peiper was held by those who served with him. Regardless of what he did or didn't do, he was somebody who was well respected by his men.

The *Birmingham Daily Gazette* of Monday 24 December 1956 reported on the release from custody of Joachim Peiper:

> Former SS Colonel Joachim Peiper, condemned to death ten years ago for his role in the Malmedy massacre of 142 American prisoners of war, was reportedly in seclusion at his family home in Baden-Baden yesterday after his release from Landsberg war crimes prison.
>
> Peiper's death sentence was commuted to life imprisonment in 1951 and later reduced to 35 years. The decision to parole him was made by a mixed German-Allied review board which does not make public its findings.

When taking into account the despicable crimes that Peiper was convicted of, it is extremely hard to understand how or why his death sentence was ever commuted to life imprisonment. At least the families of the American prisoners of war who were murdered by Peiper and his men during the course of the war, but especially at Malmedy, knew he would spend the rest of his life in prison. To see him being released after serving just eleven years must have been extremely hard for them to accept, especially as there was no official explanation as to how this decision had been reached.

Peiper's early release from prison was possibly even more confusing than that of his boss Sepp Dietrich more than a year earlier. Dietrich had been the commander of the 'Leibstandarte Adolf Hitler', he would go on to die of a heart attack, aged 74, at his home in Ludwigsburg, Germany.

Looking back at Peiper's release from prison, even from the distance of some sixty-five years, it still seems an extraordinary decision to have made, given that initially his war crimes were deemed to have been grotesque enough for him to be sentenced to death.

Chapter Nine

Peiper's Interview: 7 September 1945

The following is a record of an interview conducted with Joachim Peiper on 7 September 1945 by Major Kenneth W. Hechler of the United States Army at Freising, Germany.

- Title: 1 SS Panzer Regiment (11–24 December 1944).
- Source: Obst. (W-SS) Peiper, Joachim.
- Position: Commander, 1 SS Panzer Regiment, 1 SS Panzer Division.
- Date: 7 September 1945.
- Place: Freising, Germany.
- Interviewer: Major Kenneth W. Hechler.
- Circumstances: Obst. Peiper is a very arrogant, typical SS man, thoroughly imbued with the Nazi philosophy. He is very proud of his regiment and division and is inclined to make derogatory remarks about other units. He is possibly frightened about his future disposition. As soon as it became apparent that our conversation would be confined to military tactics and not his war crimes, he opened up. He speaks good English and took particular delight in correcting the interpreter. Physically, he is not as tall as published reports indicate.

Overall Condition of the Regiment Prior to the Offensive

(Q) What was the condition of your division immediately prior to the launching of the Ardennes Offensive?

(A) It was badly mangled in the Normandy fighting and in the retreat across France. Before the Ardennes Offensive, we had about two months to reorganize our troops in the Minden area of Westphalia.

(Q) What new troops did you receive during this re-organization period?

(A) We got about 3,500 new combat troops, bringing the division up to full T/O strength of 22,000 men.

(Q) How good were the new troops which you received?
(A) Pretty good considering the state of the German reinforcements assigned at that time.

(Q) What new materiel did you receive prior to the Ardennes Offensive?
(A) We got many new tanks directly from the assembly line. However, the regiment was supposed to have one battalion of Mark IVs and one battalion of Panzer tanks, and, not having enough tanks, I organized one battalion with a mixture of two companies of Mark IVs and two companies of Panzer tanks. To compensate for the shortage of tanks, my regiment was further reinforced with a battalion of Tiger tanks which had formerly been corps troops. Therefore, the regiment finally consisted of one battalion of mixed Panther and Mark IV tanks, one battalion of Tiger tanks, and one battalion of SS personnel without tanks. My regiment was the panzer regiment of 1 SS Panzer Division; the other two were infantry regiments.

(Q) How many additional tanks did you receive as reinforcements during the period when you re-organized in the Minden area?
(Q) Prior to coming to Westphalia we had about fifty tanks. We received about two hundred additional tanks during the period of re-equipment.

First Inkling of the Offensive

(Q) When did you first hear about the plans to launch an offensive in the Ardennes?
(A) Unofficially, I deduced the fact five days before the start of the offensive. Officially, I was informed two days before it began on 14 December 1944.

(Q) How did you deduce it unofficially?
(A) Kraemer, Chief of Staff of Sixth SS Panzer Army, asked me on 11 December 1944 what I thought about the possibilities of an attack in the Eifel region, and how much time it would take a tank regiment to proceed 80 kilometres in one night. Feeling that it was not a good idea to decide the answer to such a question merely by looking at a map, I made a test run of 80 kilometres with a Panzer tank myself, driving down the route Euskirchen, Muenstereifel, Blankenheim.

(Q) What conclusions did you reach as a result of this test run?
(A) If I had a free road to myself, I could make 80 kilometres in one night. Of course, with an entire division, that was a different question.

(Q) Do you believe that Kraemer meant to give away the plan to you?
(A) He actually didn't, but it was rather obvious what he was up to.

(Q) When did you move out of Westphalia?
(A) About three weeks before the Ardennes Offensive, our unit was moved into Army reserve 12 kilometres east of Dueren, north of Euskirchen.

(Q) Were you able to accomplish anything in training your unit between the time that Kraemer tipped you off about the impending plans and 16 December 1944?
(A) I could give them a few tips about how to drive tanks through mountainous terrain and over icy roads, but no other training or instructions were possible, because the American forces were then attacking in the Aachen–Dueren area, and we had to remain on the alert as Sixth SS Panzer Army reserve.

(Q) Could you make any personal reconnaissance in the Eifel area in advance of the offensive?
(A) No, because movement in the Eifel territory was strictly forbidden.

Plans and Preparations for the Offensive

(Q) What was the first conference held after your arrival in the new assembly area?
(A) Before noon on 14 December 1944, I was called to Tondorf, the command post of 1 SS Panzer Division, where Oberst Mohnke, the division commander, announced the whole plan for the offensive and read the detailed corps order assigning various routes and fixing the morning of 16 December 1944 as D-Day.

(Q) What divisions did you have in I SS Panzer Corps?
(A) The 1 and 12 SS Panzer Divisions; 2 Panzer Division was in the corps to our south.

(Q) What additional troops did you have assigned to your division especially for the offensive?
(A) We had one anti-aircraft regiment with 88mm guns, one additional engineer battalion, and one battalion of corps artillery with 150mm and 210mm guns. [Probably 150mm and 210mm howitzers. There was no German 210mm gun, and the 150mm gun was not normally in corps artillery.]

(Q) What was the purpose and mission of the additional engineer battalion?
(A) It was attached primarily for repairing bridges.

(Q) What particular bridge did they work on the most?
(A) The railroad bridge northwest of Losheim.

(Q) Any additional troops attached?
(A) After 3 FS [Fallschirmjäger] Division got stuck following the start of the offensive, one parachute regiment was attached to our unit. We also had at the start of the offensive special 'Skorzeny' units of 150 Panzer Brigade. Each combat team had such a group. They consisted of five hundred men, twenty General Sherman [M4] tanks, a few German tanks, thirty 2½ ton trucks, and thirty to fifty jeeps.

(Q) Where had all this American equipment been obtained?
(A) Much of it had been captured during the invasion and had stayed with various units up until October 1944, when a general order was issued to turn in all captured equipment.

(Q) Did you have any tactical control over this 'Skorzeny' group?
(A) None whatsoever.

(Q) What did you think of the value of the performance of the 'Skorzeny' group during the offensive?
(A) They might just as well have stayed at home, because they were never near the head of the column where they planned to be.

(Q) What indication of the routes was given at the division conference?
(A) Each commanding officer, the commander of the reconnaissance battalion, the commanders of the two infantry regiments, and myself got a marked map showing the routes of advance.

(Q) What area of advance was planned for 1 SS Panzer Division?
(A) Hitler Jugend [12 SS Panzer] Division was on our north, and 2 Panzer Division was on the south. We were ordered to follow this route: Schmidtheim, Dahlem, Kronenburg, Hallschlag, Scheid, Losheim, Losheimergraben, Huenningen, Honsfeld, Hepscheid, Moderscheid,

Schoppen, Ondenval, Thirimont, Ligneuville, Pont, Trois-Ponts, Werbomont, Ouffet, Seny, Tinlot, Stree, and Huy.

(Q) How good was this route compared with the routes of the divisions to your north and south?

(A) The roads assigned to the two divisions on my flanks followed main routes and were very good. The roads assigned to my division were generally known to be bad, but there were few bridges along the way.

(Q) Did you not object?

(A) I immediately pointed out that these roads were not for tanks, but were for bicycles, but they wouldn't even discuss it. They said it was the Führer's order that I should take that route.

(Q) What routes of advance were assigned for 12 SS Panzer Division and 2 Panzer Division?

(A) I did not know the route planned for 2 Panzer Division. In general, 12 SS Panzer Division planned to use the route Buellingen, Butgenbach, Waimes, Malmedy, Spa, Louveigne, Meuse River.

(Q) What additional instructions or advice were you given at the division conference?

(A) They said that my combat team in the centre was to have the decisive role in the offensive. I was not to bother about my flanks but was to drive rapidly to the Meuse River, making full use of the element of surprise.

It was further announced that two train loads of gasoline urgently needed for the offensive had not arrived, and, accordingly, orders were issued to all the units to supply themselves with captured gasoline.

(Q) Did you know where to expect to find this captured gasoline?

(A) Our division intelligence officer had a situation map purporting to show your supply installations. We believed from that map that we could capture gasoline at Buellingen and Stavelot.

(Q) Did you realize that you came within 300 yards of a three million gallon gasoline dump at Spa?

(A) [With a typical gesture Obst. Peiper shrugged his shoulders, smiled rather arrogantly, and said in English, 'I am sorry.' He didn't know of the existence of the gasoline dump.]

(Q) Did you have enough ammunition for the offensive?
(A) I obtained some ammunition myself in Euskirchen, and we had enough to last up until the fourth or fifth day.

(Q) Did you have any other shortages?
(A) No.

(Q) What else occurred at the division meeting?
(A) The division commander repeated most of Hitler's speech of 12 December 1944 to division commanders.

(Q) What did you do following the meeting?
(A) I sat down and decided how to organize my own combat team. I decided that my column would be about 25 kilometres long, and the vehicles would proceed at medium speed. It was impossible for the vehicles in the rear to overtake those in the front because of the bad roads. Therefore, all combat elements had to be placed in the front of the column. In order to provide maximum speed and power, I decided that my armoured half-tracks would proceed as fast as possible until they met resistance and then the tanks would come up to destroy the resistance, following which the half-tracks would again advance. I expected that if all went well I would need only Mark IVs and Panzers to proceed through the mountains and to reach the Meuse River, with one panzer company. Then I could move up the heavy Tiger tanks later. [The exact meaning of the last two sentences is unknown.]

(Q) Did you honestly expect to reach the Meuse River in one day?
(A) [Obst. Peiper paused for a brief period before answering and wrinkled his brow.] If our own infantry had broken through by 0700 as originally planned, my answer is 'yes', I think we might have reached the Meuse in one day.

(Q) What happened following your initial plans on 14 December 1944?
(A) On the afternoon of 14 December 1944, I drove over to confer with the commander of 12 Volks Grenadier Division, whose infantry was supposed to crack the initial line. We developed a joint plan. General Major Engel, commander of 12 Volks Grenadier Division, explained that he hoped to achieve the initial penetration by 0700 hours. I then asked General Major Engel to clear the main road of mines in the area of Losheim.

(Q) What else did General Major Engel tell you of his plans for the attack of 12 Volks Grenadier Division?

(A) He said that he had a heavy artillery concentration ready to destroy the American front line positions. He then said that he would attack with two regiments and actually reach Losheim by 0700 hours.

(Q) What else did you do on 14 December 1944?

(A) Merely general preparations, such as looking up supply routes.

(Q) When was the next conference?

(A) At 1100 on 15 December 1944 there was a conference at I SS Panzer Corps, consisting of the division commanders, the commanders of all the combat teams, and Skorzeny. Generalleutnant (W-SS) Preiss, the corps commander, gave a short 'pep' talk explaining the importance of the offensive; the chief of staff, General [actually Ostbf.] Lehmann repeated the attack order, announced that the expected gasoline had not yet arrived, but that the Führer had insisted that the offensive start on 16 December 1944, notwithstanding.

(Q) What did you think happened to that gasoline?

(A) Oh, I guess it was delayed, re-routed, and may have arrived later on in some other area, but we never saw it.

Following this, I had a conference of my own commanders, plus Skorzeny's deputy and eight or nine of his representatives. I explained the plan and its importance, that there were three main spearheads in our area, and that, of course, my combat team would be the first to reach the Meuse River. Then I explained the route to be taken, the march order, and the time each unit was to pass the IP (one kilometre southwest of Schmidtheim). Then I announced the signal SOP, and assigned wave lengths.

(Q) Was there anything unusual about your signal SOP?

(A) The only unusual thing was that the distances involved were cut in half because of the necessity for the radio waves to travel through mountainous territory.

(Q) What other orders or instructions did you issue?

(A) I issued orders against firing into small groups of the enemy and forbidding looting. I ordered this because we could not afford to lose time. I then questioned Hardecka, Skorzeny's deputy, on the mission of his group. Hardecka explained that this group would try to overtake the leading tanks as soon as possible, would then infiltrate to cause confusion among the American troops, would drop off fake MPs to direct American traffic, seize command posts, centres of communication, and a bridge over the Meuse River at either Huy or Ombret Rausa with a single coup.

(Q) What special precautions did Skorzeny's men take to protect themselves against being fired on by German troops?

(A) Tanks were to point their guns at nine o'clock and to leave them in that position throughout the journey, without any shooting at first. All soldiers were to take off their steel helmets. All vehicles had small yellow triangles in the rear.

Beginning of the Attack

(Q) How did the attack proceed on 16 December 1944?

(A) The route which we actually took was as follows: Schmidtheim, through to the railroad bridge northwest of Losheim, the same as the original plan; then we backtracked and took a secondary road to Lanzerath then through the woods in a north westerly direction to Honsfeld; Buellingen; Richelsbusch; then along the planned route through Ligneuville; then through Pont; Stavelot; Trois-Ponts; La Gleize and Stoumont.

The infantry was to open a gap through the MLR [Main Line of Resistance], and we were then to break through. At 0500 the infantry jumped off. The drive was poor, and the infantry had to bypass numerous nests of resistance which caused considerable trouble after they had been bypassed. When we started, we found that these nests of resistance also caused us quite a bit of trouble. There were many mines in the roads also.

(Q) How strong was the resistance of the American infantry?

(A) Your 99th Infantry Division put up very light resistance. In fact, the resistance was so light that it was a pity to have wasted so much artillery on them.

(Q) Where did you go when the attack started?

(A) At 0500 I moved to the command post of General Major Engel to observe his attack, in order to estimate the proper moment for launching my own push.

(Q) What did you see?

(A) Oh, I didn't see very much except the messages coming in to General Major Engel's headquarters, explaining where the infantry was fighting, and from them I could estimate when to commit my unit. It turned out I was actually at General Major Engel's command post until 1400 on 16 December 1944.

(Q) What held you up?

(A) There was a blown bridge out in 'no man's land', northwest of Losheim. This bridge had been blown by the Germans in their previous retreat from this area. Another delay occurred when either corps or army ordered the division artillery to move up farther after the infantry had broken through. Since the division artillery was a horse-drawn artillery regiment, it clogged up the roads. This was a completely idiotic idea, inasmuch as the regiment did no firing. From 1400 to 1900, I went down to the bridge to regulate traffic and tried to restore order. The bridge was not ready for use until 1930, and my combat team started at 1600 hours.

(Q) How could you get through if the roads were clogged?

(A) I ordered my vehicles to push through rapidly and to run down anything in the road ruthlessly. I finally found a detour around the bridge, a deep cut in the terrain, and reached Losheim at 1930 hours. There I received a radio message from division that the next railroad bridge could not be used, and that the engineers could not get up to it. I was told then to drive to Lanzerath, where I should meet elements of the parachute regiment of 3 Fallschirmjäger Division. This regiment had attempted to attack through the woods west of Lanzerath towards Honsfeld and had been repelled three times. I received orders to take over this regiment and to attack.

(Q) What was your objective?

(A) Obviously Honsfeld.

(Q) Did you have any difficulty?

(A) It was difficult to find my way out of Losheim because of the German and American mines. I lost five tanks and the same number of other armoured vehicles before reaching Lanzerath at midnight.

(Q) What happened at Lanzerath?

(A) There I had a conference with the commanding officer of the parachute regiment, an Oberst (I was at that time an Oberstleutnant). I asked him for all the information that he had on the enemy situation. His answer was that the woods were heavily fortified, and that scattered fire from prepared 'pill boxes' plus mines in the road were holding up his advance. He told me that it was impossible to attack under these circumstances. I asked him if he had personally reconnoitred the American positions in the woods, and he replied that he had received the information from one of his battalion commanders. I asked the battalion commander, and he said that he had got the information from a Hauptmann in his battalion. I called the Hauptmann, and he averred that he had not personally seen the American advances [forces?] but it had been 'reported to him'. At this point I became very angry and ordered the parachute regiment to give me one battalion, and I would lead the breakthrough.

I ordered my troops to deploy and be ready to attack at 0400 hours. After a conference at 0100 on 17 December 1944, I organized the attack as follows: two Panzer tanks lead the column as the point, followed by a series of armoured half-tracks and then a mixture of Panzer and M4 tanks. Strangely enough, we broke through the area without firing a shot and found it completely unoccupied.

At dawn we arrived at Honsfeld and captured a large American group still asleep. In all, our booty consisted of 50 reconnaissance vehicles, including half-tracks, about eighty 2½ ton trucks, and fifteen or sixteen anti-tank guns. One kilometre northwest of Honsfeld we received some small arms fire, but this didn't make us unhappy because although there was a slight delay, it allowed rear vehicles to close up.

(Q) How long were you delayed at this point?

(A) About half to three-quarters of an hour, allowing the parachute elements to close up. Most of them rode up on the rear tanks of my column.

Judging by the noise to our right I concluded that 12 SS Panzer Division was advancing slower than their original schedule, so I decided to take their road.

(Q) Did you communicate this fact to division?

(A) Throughout, we had no communication with division which meant anything. The first message that I received was at 0800 on 17 December

1944, asking me why the Leibstandarte ['Leibstandarte-SS Adolf Hitler', honorary title given to 1 SS Panzer Division] had not gotten started.

(Q) Where did you decide to change your route?

(A) At a small farm just on the outskirts of Honsfeld. One other thing which influenced my decision was the knowledge that an American gasoline dump probably existed at Buellingen, and we were already running low on gasoline. We drove on to Buellingen without any resistance, and there overran an American liaison plane group, destroying twelve L-5s. There was a slight delay when ground personnel at the liaison strip tried to stop us with a few machine guns.

(Q) Did you find the gasoline you were looking for?

(A) Of course. We captured 200,000 litres in Buellingen and used fifty American prisoners to fill all of our tanks. This was a lucky break, because by the time we had reached Losheim, we had used up as much gasoline in 25 kilometres as we would normally have used in covering 50 kilometres, on account of the mountainous terrain in the Eifel.

Shortly after we captured Buellingen, the American artillery laid a barrage on the town at about 0930 on 17 December 1944, causing some casualties.

From Buellingen, we drove southwest toward Moderscheid. The only difficulty here was the road through the woods, where many of our vehicles got stuck in the mud. We surprised a very small American garrison in Moderscheid.

(Q) By now did you feel that you had achieved a clean breakthrough?

(A) Yes, this was a clean breakthrough, and we continued with very little opposition. Every now and then a few stray jeeps would enter our main route of advance from side roads, apparently not realizing that we had penetrated that far. A short distance north of Thirimont, our tank point fired at an American convoy proceeding along the road from Malmedy to Ligneuville.

(Q) Was this still part of 99th Infantry Division (US)?

(A) No, this was a field artillery observation battalion.

(Q) What happened?

(A) Eleven to fifteen of their trucks were destroyed, and we moved through their convoy with little difficulty and pushed into Ligneuville. We had information there was an American command post in Ligneuville, but we got there too late and only captured their lunch. This was between twelve and one o'clock on 17 December 1944. However, we met heavy resistance just outside of Ligneuville. There we encountered American tanks for the first time and lost one Panzer and two other armoured vehicles.

(Q) What did you estimate were the American losses at this point?

(A) Two Shermans, one M10 tank destroyer, a few machine guns, and a few PWs.

Pushing through Ligneuville was quite difficult for tanks, inasmuch as there were many curves in the road.

The Battle for Stavelot

(Q) Sepp Dietrich says that Sixth SS Panzer Army lost many tanks due to mechanical difficulties. Did you have any trouble along this line?

(A) We lost only five or six tanks due to motor difficulties. In many cases the air conditioning broke down, or sometimes the brakes would not work. I hear that 12 SS Panzer Division had a lot of trouble with its tanks.

At 1600 on 17 December 1944 we reached the area of Stavelot, which was heavily defended. We could observe heavy traffic moving from Malmedy towards Stavelot, and Stavelot itself seemed clogged up completely with several hundred trucks. That night we attempted to capture Stavelot, but the terrain presented great difficulties. The only approach was the main road, and the ground to the left of the road fell very sharply, and to the right of the road rose very sharply. There was a short curve just at the entrance to Stavelot where several Sherman tanks and anti-tank guns were zeroed in.

Thereupon, we shelled Stavelot with heavy infantry howitzers and mortars, resulting in great confusion within the town and the destruction of several dumps.

At the same time, I ordered one of my Mark IV tank companies to try to find a way around Stavelot through Aisomont, Wanne, and Trois-Ponts. It proceeded along a small trail which was nearly impossible to negotiate with tanks. At 1800 a counterattack circled around a high hill 800 metres east of Stavelot and hit my column from the south.

(Q) Were any tanks included in this counterattack?

(A) No, the terrain was much too difficult, and the counterattack consisted entirely of infantry. After the counterattack was repulsed, I committed more armoured infantry to attack Stavelot again. We approached the outskirts of the village but bogged down because of stubborn American resistance at the edge of Stavelot. We suffered fairly heavy losses, twenty-five to thirty casualties, from tank, anti-tank, mortar, and rifle fire. Since I did not have sufficient infantry, I decided to wait for the arrival of more infantry.

(Q) Where did you expect to get this infantry?

(A) I had one battalion of armoured infantry in my column. As darkness fell, we observed heavy American traffic all moving westward, without blackout restrictions. We fired at them up to a range of 4,800 metres with our tanks but launched no additional organized counterattacks until dawn of 18 December 1944. At dawn, I committed another armoured infantry company against Stavelot. I withdrew two Panzer tanks 200 metres from the edge of the town and instructed them to charge Stavelot at maximum speed. They drove around the curve firing rapidly. The first Panzer tank was hit, and it burned, but it had so much initial speed that it penetrated the anti-tank obstacle at the curve and damaged two Sherman tanks. The second Panzer used this opportunity to drive through and seize a bridge in Stavelot. We followed up with other vehicles, and the Americans evacuated the town, leaving some materiel.

(Q) How much?

(A) Oh, I didn't see it.

Efforts to Continue the Advance

(Q) Where did you go?

(A) We proceeded at top speed towards Trois-Ponts in an effort to seize the bridge there. We were delayed briefly by an anti-tank gun east of the bridge. We destroyed the anti-tank gun, but then the enemy blew up the bridge in our faces.

(Q) What was the importance of the bridge in Trois-Ponts; in other words, what do you think you might have been able to do if you captured the bridge intact?

(A) If we had captured the bridge at Trois-Ponts intact and had had enough fuel, it would have been a simple matter to drive through to the Meuse River early that day.

Blocked at Trois-Ponts, we continued on to La Gleize where we encountered little resistance. There was another important bridge near Cheneux, which we prevented from being blown. However, in the afternoon of 18 December 1944 we had a bad break when the weather cleared and American fighter-bombers came over. We lost two to three tanks and five armoured half-tracks. The tanks blew up in the road, and the road was too narrow to bypass them, thus causing additional delay. About 1800 on 18 December 1944 we moved up towards our old route of advance near Habiemont and started to cross the Lienne River. Just when we were starting to cross, this bridge also was blown up. I sent one of my tank companies on a reconnaissance mission to find another bridge north of this point. Elements advanced over a newly discovered bridge and then were ambushed and suffered heavy casualties. It was then reported that the bridge was not heavy enough for our tanks. Not being able to find another bridge, it was decided to turn north to Stoumont and La Gleize. After reaching La Gleize, another group reconnoitred towards Stoumont. It was reported that Stoumont was strongly held and that powerful American forces were moving from Spa towards Stoumont.

Failure of the Offensive

(Q) Did you observe any difference in quality of American troops in this sector?

(A) Decidedly. We were now confronting elements of your 30th Infantry Division and 82nd Airborne Division, who fought far more savagely than 99th Infantry Division (US). We decided to hold the bridge southwest of La Gleize, since it might prove important later on, and to attack Stoumont. At daylight on 19 December 1944, we attacked Stoumont with one battalion of armoured infantry and one company of parachutists attacking on both sides of the road, supported by tank fire. Again because of the terrain, tanks were unable to leave the road. Strong fire from Stoumont and heavy flanking fire from the north from your 30th Infantry Division checked our attempts to enter Stoumont. However, we used the same technique of sending in two to three tanks at maximum speed, and eventually broke into and cleared out the village, and then pushed westward to seize a bridge west of Stoumont. This was about as much as we could do with the gasoline that we had.

From then on, events turned rapidly against us. The same day, the commanding officer of the reconnaissance battalion reported that

Stavelot had been retaken. As our infantry had been pushed to the eastern edge of the town, I immediately ordered him to attack from the west and clear Stavelot.

On 19 December 1944 three counterattacks launched at Stoumont were repelled. However, we began to realize that we had insufficient gasoline to cross the bridge west of Stoumont. Therefore, we ordered the forces west of Stoumont to withdraw to the town.

On 20 December 1944 we tried to attack again, with little success. American troops attacked us from northeast of La Gleize and at the same time attacked Cheneux, where we had left a group to protect the bridge. Realizing that we were weak at La Gleize, Stoumont and Cheneux, and endangered at all three points, we decided to abandon Stoumont that night. A small counterattack covered our withdrawal from Stoumont. After Cheneux had been captured and recaptured twice, we abandoned it and retreated to La Gleize on the night of 20 December 1944.

(Q) What were the orders that you received from division headquarters during this period?

(A) [Obst. Peiper sniffed cynically.] I got one message that I should report immediately the location of my dressing stations for the wounded, and that unless I reported the amount of gas I still had on hand, I could not hope for any additional gasoline.

(Q) Were you able to maintain radio contact and inform division of your whereabouts?

(A) We had no regular radio contact with division, but division knew of our whereabouts by listening in to the American radios.

(Q) What indication did you get that the entire Ardennes Offensive had failed in a larger sense?

(A) The first indication we had was a message on 23 December 1944 at 1700 ordering us to break out toward the east with our vehicles and men. When I received that message I realized that the only chance was to break out without any vehicles and wounded. Accordingly on 24 December 1944, at 0100, we abandoned all our vehicles and started walking back.

(Q) What were your losses?

(A) We had to leave over three hundred in La Gleize, and they were probably captured. Only eight hundred men got out.

(Q) If you had to launch this offensive again, what measures would you execute differently, both in the higher planning and within your own regiment?

(A) It soon became apparent that the real aim of the Ardennes Offensive was not to reach Antwerp, but simply to disturb American preparations and delay the American winter offensive for two months. This should have been made clear by the higher command at the start of the counteroffensive. There are certain definite things that I would do differently:

- Institute a speedier system of supplying gasoline.
- Have no artillery preparation and keep the horse-drawn artillery from clogging the roads.
- Attack with combat teams and tanks at the same time as the infantry. An unsupported infantry attack wastes too much time.
- Reduce the length of each column, and instead of three columns use twenty; then upon finding the softest spot, all columns should concentrate on this point.
- Use more infantry on tanks.
- Take along a bridging unit with each armoured point.
- Make each combat team completely self-sufficient.
- Put a general at each street corner to regulate traffic. [Obst. Peiper indicated that there were two good reasons for such a move, and one of them was not traffic control.]

What is quite unbelievable about this interrogation is that, given Peiper was charged with war crimes, the interrogator did not ask him one single difficult question about the events that took place at Malmedy, including the most important question of all: whether he had murdered, or ordered the murder of, unarmed American prisoners of war. Many of the questions appeared almost irrelevant.

Chapter Ten

Peiper's Trial

A General Military Court of the United States Army met at Dachau, Germany, on 16 May 1946. On trial were seventy-three members of the SS.

It was a crowded court room, as there were seven interpreters, nine reporters, a number of court staff, military security personnel, members of the defence counsel, and the prosecution team in addition to the defendants and their legal representatives. Of the defendants, Helmut Haas, Herbert Losenski, Werner Pedersen, and Emil Hergeth, were not present.

The Members of the Court as appointed by special order of the Third United States Army, which was dated 10 May 1946, were:

Brigadier General Josiah T. Dalbey.
Colonel Paul H. Weiland.
Colonel Lucien S. Berry.
Colonel James G. Watkins.
Colonel Wilfred H. Steward.
Colonel Raymond C. Conder.
Colonel A.H. Rosenfeld.

The Trial Judge Advocate and his Assistants were:

Lieutenant Colonel Burton F. Ellis. (Trial Judge Advocate).
Lieutenant Colonel Homer B. Crawford.
Captain Raphael Shumacker.
1st Lieutenant Robert E. Byrne.
Mr Morris Elowitz.

The defendants were:

SS-Obergruppenführer Josef Dietrich. Originally sentenced to life imprisonment but released from prison on 22 October 1955. Died in Ludswigberg on 21 April 1966.

SS Brigadeführer Fritz Kramer. Originally sentenced to ten years imprisonment, but released on 23 January 1952. He died on 23 June 1959, in Hamburg-Ohlsdorf.

SS Gruppenführer Hermann August Friedrich Priess. Originally sentenced to life imprisonment, but released on 16 June 1954 after having served just eight years. He died in Ahrensburg, Germany on 2 March 1985.

SS Standartenführer Joachim Peiper. Initially sentenced to death for his crimes, was commuted to a life sentence on 31 January 1951. He was released in 1956 after having served just ten years.

SS-Obersturmführer Friedrich Christ. Initially sentenced to death for war crimes, this was commuted to life imprisonment on 28 March 1949, before he was finally released on 31 July 1955. He died on 13 April 2001 in Euskirchen, Germany.

SS Sturmbannführer Josef Diefenthal. Initially sentenced to death, which was commuted to life imprisonment. He was released from prison on 22 October 1955.

Diefenthal was recommended for the Knights Cross, which he was awarded on 15 February 1945, for his role during the 'armoured groups' push to the Ambleve River and which included the actions at Malmedy and Stoumont. His recommendation read:

> SS-Hauptsturmführer Diefenthal has outstandingly distinguished himself in all previous campaigns. In all situations he was the model and champion of his battalion through his energy, liveliness and astonishing resilience.
>
> Diefenthal had a major role to play in the successes of the armoured group during its thrust to the Ambleve river in the time period 16-24 December 1944.
>
> On the 18 December 1944, as the armoured group was located before Stoumont, a forward advance by our forces no longer seemed to be possible. The American blocking formations fought bitterly to cover their withdrawal from Malmedy, and were aided by the extremely difficult terrain. In this context the enemy launched a counterattack against elements of the armoured group that were located on the road, however they were repulsed. After this Diefenthal immediately took charge of the situation and at once decided to pursue the fleeing enemy with his battalion. Fighting at their head, he and his men penetrated into the hotly contested village. They utilized the existing panic to thrust through to the bridge, prevent its destruction and hold on to it despite the heavy losses incurred until help from the rear arrived.
>
> By this decisive feat of arms Diefenthal laid the groundwork for the continued advance.

> His bravery, personality and leadership have been a solid example for the entire Kampfgruppe.
>
> In light of his singular performance [it is recommended] that Diefenthal be awarded the Knight's Cross to the Iron Cross.

SS-Hauptsturmführer Oskar Klingelhofer. Initially sentenced to death by the American military tribunal, later commuted to life imprisonment, before he was released from prison on 23 December 1953, after having served just seven years.

SS-Sturmbannführer Gustav Knittel. Initially sentenced to life imprisonment, but released from prison on 9 December 1953.

SS-Hauptsturmführer Hans Gruhle. Sentenced to twenty years' imprisonment, but was released from prison on 6 February 1952, after having served less than six years.

SS-Obersturmführer Benoni Junker. Initially sentenced to death, later commuted to life imprisonment. Was released on 11 September 1951.

SS-Unterscharführer Oswald Siegmund. Initially sentenced to death, commuted to life imprisonment on 20 March 1948.

SS-Obersturmführer Manfred Coblenz. Initially sentenced to life imprisonment. Was released after having served just five years, on 8 September 1951.

SS-Unterscharführer Otto Wichmann was sentenced to just ten years imprisonment.

SS-Sturmmann Georg Fleps. Sentenced to death at his Dachau trial on 20 March 1948, subsequently commuted to life imprisonment in August 1951. Fleps was Romanian by birth.

SS-Oberscharführer Roman Clotten. Sentenced to ten years' imprisonment.

SS-Rottenführer Theodor Rauh. Initially sentenced to death, but this was commuted to life imprisonment on 20 March 1948.

SS-Sturmmann Gustav Adolf Sprenger. Sentenced to death, later commuted to life imprisonment. He was released from prison on 10 April 1948.

SS-Sturmmann Fritz Eckmann. Had served as a 'funker' or tank radio operator, was initially sentenced to death for his war crimes, which was subsequently commuted to life imprisonment. He was released on 10 April 1948.

Grenadier Heinz Gerhard Gödicke. Sentenced to life imprisonment.

SS-Obersturmführer Erich Rumpf. Sentenced to death, commuted to life imprisonment on 29 March 1949. Released from prison on 1 October 1954.

SS-Sturmmann Friedel Kies. Initially sentenced to death, later commuted to life imprisonment.

SS-Hauptsturmführer Georg Preuss. Initially sentenced to death, commuted to life imprisonment on 17 March 1949. Released from Landsberg Prison on 30 November 1956. Ernst Kilat, who had served under Preuss, testified against him, stating that, as company commander, Preuss had ordered his men to kill all Belgian civilians encountered by the unit. In 1948, Kilat was tried and found guilty of murdering Belgian civilians in Luttich. During his trial at Dachau, it was shown he had ordered one of his men to shoot a captured American prisoner of war, for no other reason than he liked the trousers and a ring that he was wearing

SS-Rottenführer Erwin Szyperski. Served with the 3rd SS Panzer Regiment. Found guilty and sentenced to life imprisonment.

SS-Untersturmführer, Hans Hennecke. Served with the 1st Company, SS Panzer Regiment 1, LSSAH. Originally sentenced to death, commuted to life imprisonment on 20 March 1948. Released on 23 December 1953, after having served just seven years.

SS-Hauptscharführer August Tonk. Served with the 1st SS Panzer Regiment. Initially sentenced to death, later commuted to life imprisonment.

SS-Sturmbannführer Kurt Sickel. Sentenced to death, subsequently commuted to life imprisonment. Released on 17 May 1954, having served just eight years in prison.

Grenadier Wolfgang Richter. Sentenced to life imprisonment, but despite this was released from prison on 10 April 1948.

SS-Rottenführer Max Hammerer. Originally sentenced to death. Commuted to life imprisonment on 20 March 1948.

SS-Sturmmann Hans Trettin. Sentenced to life imprisonment.

SS-Unterscharführer Axel Rodenburg. Originally sentenced to death. On 20 March 1948, this was commuted to twenty-five years imprisonment.

SS-Rottenführer Siegfried Jäkel. Originally sentenced to death. Later commuted to life imprisonment.

SS-Rottenführer Erich Werner. Sentenced to life imprisonment, commuted to 15 years on 20 March 1948.

SS-Sturmmann Willi Braun. Sentenced to life imprisonment.

SS-Rottenführer Ernst Goldschmidt. Sentenced to death, later commuted to life imprisonment.

SS-Obersturmführer Heinz Tomhardt. Sentenced to death subsequently commuted to life imprisonment. He was released from prison on 6 February 1952 after having served less than six years.

SS-Untersturmführer Arndt Fischer. Sentenced to fifteen years imprisonment but was released after less than six years on 28 March 1951.

SS-Unterscharführer Erich Otto Maute. Sentenced to death, which was later commuted to life imprisonment. He was released from prison on 10 April 1948, after having served just two years of his sentence.

Grenadier Fritz Gebauer. Sentenced to life imprisonment.

SS-Oberscharführer Hubert Huber. Initially sentenced to death, commuted to life imprisonment. Released 29 January 1957.

SS-Sturmmann Georg Kotzur. Sentenced to life imprisonment. Died on 11 August 1948 in prison.

SS-Sturmmann Max Rieder. Initially sentenced to death, commuted to life imprisonment. Released less than two years after the Dachau trial on 10 April 1948.

SS-Hauptscharführer Willi Heinz Hendel. Initially sentenced to death, commuted to life imprisonment.

SS-Hauptscharführer Paul Hermann Ochmann. Initially sentenced to death, commuted to life imprisonment on 20 March 1948. Released from prison aeven years later on 16 June 1955.

SS-Unterscharführer Willi von Chamier. Sentenced to life imprisonment for his part in the Malmedy massacre.

SS-Sturmmann Rolf Ritzer. Sentenced to life imprisonment.

SS-Unterscharführer Hans Kurt Hillig. Sentenced to ten years imprisonment.

SS-Unterscharführer Rudolf Schwambach. Sentenced to death, later commuted to life imprisonment.

Grenadier Fritz Rau. Sentenced to life imprisonment.

SS-Sturmmann Joachim Hofmann. Sentenced to death, later commuted to life imprisonment.

SS-Obersturmführer Werner Sternebeck. Initially sentenced to death, later commuted to life imprisonment. Released from prison on 20 March 1948.

SS-Sturmmann Herbert Stock. Sentenced to life imprisonment.

SS-Sturmmann Arnold Mikolascheck. Sentenced to life imprisonment.

SS-Untersturmführer Heinz Rehagel. Sentenced to death, commuted to life imprisonment. Released from prison on 3 March 1954.

SS-Rottenführer Edmund Tomczak. Sentenced to life imprisonment.

SS-Sturmmann Marcel Boltz. Acquitted – but his is a strange story. During his trial Boltz testified that he had machine-gunned 'mercy shots' into wounded American soldiers during the Malmedy massacre. He was serving with the 3rd Group, 2nd Platoon of the 3rd Panzer Pioneer Company, 1st Pioneer Battalion. A statement made by Boltz included the admission that on either 13 or 14 of December 1944, he was present when Untersturmführer

Sette, the leader of the 1st Platoon, made a speech. Boltz claimed that during that speech Sette said, 'In the coming offensive no prisoners of war will be taken but will be shot immediately.'

It is claimed that, despite admitting machine-gunning wounded American prisoners of war, Boltz was acquitted because he was a French citizen who had been recruited to the SS after Germany annexed Alsace in 1940.

SS-Unterscharführer Anton Motzheim. Sentenced to death, later commuted to life imprisonment.

SS-Rottenführer Heinz Hofmann. Sentenced to life imprisonment, commuted on 20 March 1948 to a fifteen-year term of imprisonment.

SS-Obersturmführer Franz Sievers. Originally sentenced to death for his part in the Malmedy massacre, but on 20 March 1948 this was commuted to life imprisonment. Seven years later, on 17 August 1955, he was released from prison.

SS-Unterscharführer Hans Pletz. Sentenced to life imprisonment, commuted on 31 January 1951 to ten years imprisonment. Released from prison less than one year later on 4 January 1952.

SS-Untersturmführer Werner Kühn. Sentenced to death, later commuted to life imprisonment.

SS-Sturmmann Heinz Stickel. Initially sentenced to death for his part in the Malmedy massacre, commuted to life imprisonment. Stickel was released from prison on 10 April 1948, less than two years after the trial.

SS-Hauptsturmführer Gerd Nüske. Sentenced to life imprisonment for his part in the Malmedy massacre.

SS-Unterscharführer Paul Zwigart. Initially sentenced to death for his part in the massacre, later commuted to life imprisonment.

SS-Unterscharführer Kurt Briesemeister. Initially sentenced to death, subsequently commuted to life imprisonment.

Grenadier Heinz Friedrichs. Sentenced to life imprisonment.

SS-Oberscharführer Willi Schäfer. Sentenced to death, but on 20 March 1948 this was commuted to life imprisonment.

SS-Unterscharführer Friedel Bode. Sentenced to death, later commuted to life imprisonment.

SS-Rottenführer Armin Hecht. Sentenced to life imprisonment.

SS-Sturmmann Gustav Neve. Sentenced to death, subsequently commuted to life imprisonment.

SS-Oberscharführer Valentin Bersin. Sentenced to death, commuted to life imprisonment. His was the name on the official title of the trial: 'Malmedy Massacre Record of Trial: United States vs. Valentin Bersin et al.' Bersin's name was included in the official title of the trial papers because, alphabetically, his was the first of the seventy-three Waffen-SS defendants.

Pioneer Johann Wasenberger. Austrian by birth. Sentenced to life imprisonment.

SS-Hauptscharführer Hans Siptrott. Initially sentenced to death, later commuted to life imprisonment.

SS-Sturmmann Günther Weis. Initially sentenced to death. On 20 March 1948, this was commuted to twenty-five years imprisonment.

SS-Untersturmführer Erich Münkemer. Sentenced to death. Later commuted to life imprisonment, released from prison on 12 December 1952.

SS-Untersturmführer Rolf Roland Reiser. Sentenced to ten years imprisonment, but was released from prison less than two years after the trial, on 10 April 1948.

One of the defendants, 18-year-old Arvid Freimuth, committed suicide in his cell at Schwäbisch Hall prison, where he was being held before the trial started. The irony is that regardless of what part he had played in the massacre, ultimately he would not have been executed.

All of the defendants in the case, including Peiper, faced the charge that they were in violation of the 'laws and usages of war' in that they 'wilfully, deliberately and wrongfully permitted, encouraged, aided, abetted and participated in the killing, shooting, ill-treatment, abuse and torture of members of the Armed Forces of the United States of America, and of unarmed allied civilians'.

The defence counsel began proceedings by asking the president of the court, Brigadier General Josiah T. Dalbey, to determine if any of the court members had any prior knowledge of the facts of the case by virtue of their participation in the Ardennes Offensive, which was commonly referred to as the Battle of the Bulge, because the defence suggested that any such involvement would prejudice an individual's judgement in the case. All of the court members confirmed that they had not taken part in or been involved in any aspect of the Battle of the Bulge.

They then requested that the court members also be asked if they had any prior knowledge of the facts in the case from any other source which would prejudice their judgement. Once again, they confirmed that they had no such knowledge.

It seems almost impossible to contemplate that seventeen months after the Malmedy massacre had occurred – what has been claimed as the worst atrocity against members of the United States military in the European theatre of war during the course of the Second World War – it was not known by one single member of the American military establishment.

As if they hadn't asked for enough assurances from the members of the court, the defence counsel then asked if any of them had formed an opinion as to the guilt or innocence of the accused. Once again, the answer was no, they had not. The defence counsel then wanted the members asked if they were prejudiced against any or all of the defendants because they were allegedly members of the SS. The collective answer from all of the members was a resounding, 'no'.

I do not believe there was one single member of the United States Army who was not prejudice towards any and all members of the SS because of the number of atrocities they had committed during the course of the Second World War.

Defence counsel then presented the president of the court with a motion challenging the court's jurisdiction to actually put the seventy-three SS men on trial, quoting among other things what was referred to as the 'Moscow Conference', which took place in Moscow on 1 November 1943. It was attended by delegates from the United States, Russia and Great Britain. This agreement would also become enshrined in the Potsdam Declaration of September 1945. The declaration which came out of the 'Moscow Conference' was as follows:

> At the time of the granting of an armistice to any government which may be set up in Germany, those officers and men, members of the Nazi Party, who have been responsible for, or who have taken part in the above atrocities, massacres and executions will be sent back to the country in which these abominable deeds were done, in order that they may be judged and punished according to the laws of these liberated countries and of the free governments which will be erected therein.

Joachim Peiper was one of the men specifically mentioned by the defence counsel. The charge against him was that he was responsible for the shootings of prisoners of war and allied civilians by men of his company, between 16 December 1944 and 13 January 1945.

The prosecution counsel counter-argued by stating that in this particular case the offence charged was not being judged as a violation of the laws of

Belgium, but of international law. More specifically the evidence, it was claimed, showed that the murders of Belgium civilians and American soldiers were, in fact, violations of Article 2 of the Geneva Convention and Article 46 of the Hague Convention, which related to the treatment of prisoners of war and of civilians of a hostile state respectively. The prosecution further stated that if the charges were true, and had actually taken place, then the people of the civilised world, and not just Belgium, had a direct and vital interest in seeing that those responsible were punished.

To give further strength to their argument, the prosecution pointed out that no matter what agreement was reached at the Moscow Conference, nowhere did it make any allowance to provide defendants with any rights. So in the case of Peiper and his seventy-two former SS colleagues, they had no rights, legal or otherwise, to demand via their counsels that they should be tried in Belgium.

As if they hadn't put a strong enough counter argument to the defence's motion that the United States Military Tribunal had no jurisdiction to try the defendants at Dachau, the prosecution counsel delivered the equivalent of a coup de grace:

> I would like to further add that when this case was in the process of development in March of this year, permission in writing was received from the Belgian government to try at that time four or five incidents. Later on there were further developments in the case and additional offences against Belgian civilians were disclosed. Although written permission was not received from the Belgian government, the Belgian government was fully notified of what happened and they cooperated and loaned to us Germans who were prisoners of war in our custody to prove the cases which we have charged against the defendants covered by these motions. They also cooperated by assisting us in giving us witnesses who will be used to testify against the defendants covered by these motions.

The prosecution won the day and the defence counsel's motion was thrown out. But undeterred, they tried further delaying tactics by demanding that the court matters be immediately translated into German, as a number of the defendants and some the defence team could not speak or understand English. When this was agreed, one of the German members of the defence counsel, Dr Leiling, then complained about the interpreter stating that his translation was insufficient, which rather suggested that if he wasn't happy about the translation, he could in fact speak and understand English. But, maybe because there was concern that any subsequent 'positive' outcome of the case would be laid open to challenge if the defendants were not provided with every possible nicety, the interpreter was changed.

Still the defence counsel were not happy, and one of their number, a Lieutenant Wahler, again questioned the decision to deny their motion concerning jurisdiction. To add weight to their argument, he quoted comments which supported their stance made by former Judge Advocate General Colonel Windthrop in his book, *Military Law and Precedents*, which covered the topic of jurisdiction. He further quoted similar supportive material from a report written by a Harvard University Professor, Sheldon Glick, on the subject of jurisdiction in the context of their case.

After giving the defence's motion over the issue of jurisdiction due consideration, the court denied it, giving a detailed account for its reasons why.

Dr Leiling for the defence then posed another motion, quoting the Hague Convention of 1907 and the Geneva Convention of 1929, pointing out that these conventions were international treaties and therefore subject to international law. This being the case, he further added that if the alleged crimes were proven, they would be a violation of the above conventions, and according to the rules of international law, the case in question should be a matter for the sovereign States involved, and not between the victorious State and individuals of the defeated one.

The court once again considered the motion and once again denied it.

The prosecution then announced that it had a motion to drop charges against the defendants Helmuth Haas, Herbert Losenski, Werner Petersen, and Emil Hergeth, without prejudice, by reason of the fact that they were not present before the court. Not surprisingly, this was a motion which received no objection from the defence counsel.

Dr Rau, a member of the defence counsel then raised a further motion concerning the status of the defendants and how this was relevant under the terms of the Geneva Convention of 1929. He stated that his clients were not aware that they were not prisoners of war and were concerned as to the position they then found themselves in if they were not covered by the terms of the Geneva Convention.

The prosecution pointed out that this was a motion which had been raised and dismissed in previous war crimes trials held before a General Military Government Court. They also clarified that each and every one of the defendants had never technically been a prisoner of war as they had all been detained after the war and fighting had ceased, which meant that they had actually been arrested for war crimes while in Allied custody as non-combatants.

Once again the motion by the defence counsel was denied. With this being the last of their numerous motions to be thrown out, the president announced that the court was declared to be a properly constituted entity, had jurisdiction in the case, and that the trial of all of the defendants present would be conducted in open court.

Each of the defendants, in alphabetical order regardless of their rank, was then asked to stand and answer a number of basic questions. The first defendant to stand was Valentin Bersin; after he had answered the questions put to him, he became referred to as the accused number one.

Each of the defendants was asked the following:

Question. What is your full name?
Question. How old are you?
Question. Where is your home?
Question. What is your nationality?
Question. Were you ever a member of the Armed forces of the German Reich?
Question. Of what component were you a member and during what period of time?

The third defendant to be asked this set of questions was 19-year-old Marcel Boltz, who joined the SS on 10 October 1943, when he was only 17 years of age. As noted above, Boltz wasn't German, he was actually French.

The thirteenth defendant was George Fleps, who is covered elsewhere in this book. He was identified by a survivor of the Malmedy massacre as one of the SS soldiers who shot dead at least one of the American prisoners of war. He was Romanian.

Defendant number twenty-seven was Hubert Huber, an Austrian who had been a member of the SS between April 1938 and 22 December 1944.

Defendant number forty-eight, Rolf Roland Reiser, was Romanian, and had been a member of the SS between 15 July 1943, and the end of the war.

Defendant number seventy, Johann Wasenberger, was an Austrian, and had been a member of the Waffen SS for a period of ten months up until the end of 1944.

Joachim Peiper was defendant number forty-two of the seventy-three, and as we know, he had been a member of the Waffen SS from October 1934.

The seventy-three defendants were then collectively addressed by the president of the court and told their rights and what would be provided for them, which included the right to defend themselves, give oral evidence, and have any of the witnesses who spoke against them, cross-examined.

The defence then posed another motion that the trial should be split in to two. One trial to include fourteen of the defendants, who allegedly gave or published orders for prisoners of war or Allied civilians to be shot, and/or for the aiding and abetting of such orders. The second trial would deal with the remaining sixty defendants who had been charged with actually participating in the shooting and killing of prisoners of war or Allied civilians.

The reasons for making the motion were that, by the very nature of the charges, the defence of some of the offenders would, by necessity, be antagonistic to that of others. There would be an unavoidable conflict of interest among the accused, and because there would inevitably be a shifting of culpability and a casting of burden from one accused to another.

Captain Shumacker, answering for the defence, pointed out that there had already been a number of similar trials where large groups of defendants had been charged and tried together because, as in this case, they were all before the court in relation to the same allegations. With this in mind he asked that the court should refuse the defence's request for separate trials and go ahead with one trial, against all of the defendants, as had been the intention all along. The court found in favour of the prosecution.

It is interesting to note that the defence had not previously had an issue with how the trial was to go ahead, and that this appears to have been on a list of delaying tactics they were prepared to use if previous motions were refused. In the circumstances, I believe they would have had more chance of achieving two separate trials if they had made that their first motion, as it would have had more credence and appeared more genuine, rather than putting it forward as their fifth or sixth motion, which simply made it look like a desperate measure and delaying tactic.

The court was adjourned at 5.20pm on that first day, and had been taken up purely with motions by the defence; the trial proper had not yet commenced. The question is: were the defence intentionally employing delaying tactics with an ulterior motive in mind, or were the motions they were putting before the court genuine and purely for the benefit of their clients?

The second day of the case commenced at 8.30 the following morning, 17 May 1946. After it was confirmed that everybody who needed to be in attendance was present, the day's proceedings commenced. The first business of the day was when counsel for the defence announced that all of their clients would be pleading not guilty. This was immediately followed by the prosecution making their opening statement, in which they briefly outlined the evidence they intended to present to the court, including the following:

> The offensive which is referred to in this trial was known to the Germans as the Eifel Offensive. To the Americans it was more commonly referred to as the Battle of the Bulge, the Rundstedt Offensive or the Ardennes Offensive. We expect to show that for this offensive there existed a general policy to spread terror and panic, to avenge the so-called terror bombings, and to break all resistance by murdering prisoners of war and unarmed civilians.
>
> In preparation for this offensive, which started on 16 December 1944, Hitler held a meeting of his Army Commanders at Bad Nauheim on 11 or 12 December 1944, where he spoke for some three hours. In this speech Hitler stated that the Army would have to act with brutality and show no humane inhibitions; that a wave of fright and terror should precede the Army and that the enemy's resistance was to be broken with terror.
>
> We expect the evidence to show that the 6th Panzer Army, commanded by the accused Dietrich, passed on the tenor of Hitler's speech in an order to its subordinate commands in words and substance to the effect that 'considering the desperate situation of the German people, a wave of terror and fright should precede the troops; that the soldier should in this offensive recall the innumerable German victims of the bombing terror; that the enemy's resistance had to be broken by terror, that prisoners of war must be shot when the local conditions of combat should so require it'. This order was passed on down through corps, Division, and Regiment.
>
> The 1st SS Panzer Regiment commanded by the accused Peiper, passed on this order to subordinate commands in words and substance to the effect that 'this fight will be conducted stubbornly, with no regard for Allied prisoners of war who will have to be shot, if the situation makes it necessary and compels it'. This order was read to subordinate commanders who in turn passed it on down to Company Commanders who likewise passed it to lower echelons and to the troops.

This type of order had the potential to cause problems for the prosecution of war criminals, as it gave soldiers at the bottom of the chain of command the opportunity to claim that they were only following the orders they had been given by their superior officers. These were known as 'Superior Orders'.

The prosecution intended to show that on the afternoon of 15 December and during the night of 15 and 16 December 1944, at the assembly area which was in the vicinity of Blackenheim, Germany, troop meetings were held of the companies, platoons and tank groups, where these orders were given to the troops in varying degrees of boldness and callousness, depending upon the individual handing out the orders.

Some troops were even told to 'excel in the killing of prisoners of war, as well as in the fighting of others that they would fight again in the old traditional SS manner'. Others were told to make plenty of 'Rabatz', which in SS parlance meant to have plenty of fun by killing everything that came in sight. Some were even told to 'Bump off everything that came before their guns.'

All of the SS troops were warned by their officers that in the event of their capture by the enemy, the existence of these orders was not to made known.

The tactics deployed by the SS were in the main based on the military tactics of Genghis Khan. Throughout 1937, SS officers were taught the significance of the tactics deployed by him in warfare, while they were undergoing their training at SS military academies. All SS men who graduated from officer cadet school were issued with a copy of a book by Michael Prawdin, entitled *Genghis Khan and his Legacy.*

According to Prawdin, in Genghis Khan's first attack his men had to be so fierce as to instil terror and panic in their enemy, being so severe as to cause any defenders to be left paralysed with fear, thus making the local population realise that any kind of resistance was futile.

Because of the orders given to SS troops, they believed they could disregard the accepted rules of war as laid down by the Geneva Convention with impunity.

The prosecution then read out the names of the different units which made up Dietrich's 6th Panzer Army, including the 1st SS Panzer Regiment under the command of Joachim Peiper, also known as 'Combat Group Peiper'. The 6th Panzer Army was made up of two battalions of four companies each, along with a reconnaissance battalion composed of eight companies. In addition there were two companies of the 1st Panzer Pioneer (Engineer) Battalion, the 501st Heavy Tank Battalion, the 2nd Artillery Battalion, and the 68th Anti-Aircraft Battalion, as well as a number of infantry units:

1st SS Panzer Regiment, Headquarters Company.

9th Panzer Pioneer Company.

1st Panzer Battalion, which consisted of a Headquarters Company, the 1st Panzer Company, 2nd Panzer Company, 6th and 7th Panzer Companies.

2nd Panzer Grenadier Regiment.

3rd Panzer Grenadier Battalion, which consisted of a Headquarters Company, the 9th, 10th, 11th, and 12th Panzer Grenadier Companies.

3rd Panzer Grenadier Company

Of all the different elements of Dietrich's 6th Panzer Army, the prosecution had evidence to show that the alleged atrocities had specifically been carried out by officers and men of Combat Group Peiper.

The route taken by the 1st SS Panzer Regiment once the Eifel Offensive began saw them leave Blankenheim on 16 December 1944, before travelling on through the German towns and villages of Dahlem, Stadtkyll, Kronenburg, Hallschlag, Scheid, and Losheim. From there they crossed into Belgium and travelled through Lanzerath, Honsfeld, Buellingen, Schopen, Ondenval, Thirimont, and on to a crossroads just south of Malmedy, where the massacre took place. From there they travelled on to Baugnez, Ligneuville, which was known to the Germans by the name of Engelsdorf, before continuing on to Stavelot, La Gleize and finally Stoumont, where they arrived on 19 December, coming to a halt at the town's railway station. Before long they were forced to retreat to La Gleize, where they were quickly surrounded by American forces up until the night of 23/24 December. Peiper did not want to find himself in a position of having to surrender, if for no other reason than he had absolutely no idea how he and his men would be treated, unaware of whether the Americans knew of the massacre at Malmedy.

Peiper ordered his men to destroy their vehicles and make good their escape on foot to the south. In part they had been forced to take this course of action because, during their earlier advance towards Stoumont, they had failed to clear out all the American troops, a failure which had resulted in Peiper's supply lines being cut. Realising this was the case, Peiper sent his

A young, intense looking Peiper in polo neck and no hat.

Peiper at his trial at Dachau concentration camp, seated next to a translator, whilst he gives evidence.

Two American soldiers carrying the body of a dead colleague on a stretcher, who was one of those executed at Malmedy.

Peiper (fourth from left), Himmler and Franco in Spain October 1940.

Peiper and a colleague on foot on the outskirts of Malmedy.

American prisoners of war captured in the Malmedy area during the Battle of the Bulge.

Kurt Kramm, a witness and fellow ex SS member sitting next to an interpreter and the prosecuting lawyer whilst giving evidence against Peiper.

Kenneth Arhens, a survivor of the Malmedy massacre, giving evidence in the Dachau trial of Peiper and his colleagues, whilst sat next to an interpreter.

Soldiers from the 333rd Field Artillery Battalion, some of whom were murdered by the SS at Wereth, Belgium in December 1944.

Joachim Peiper (standing) at his trial at Dachau concentration camp on 16 May 1946.

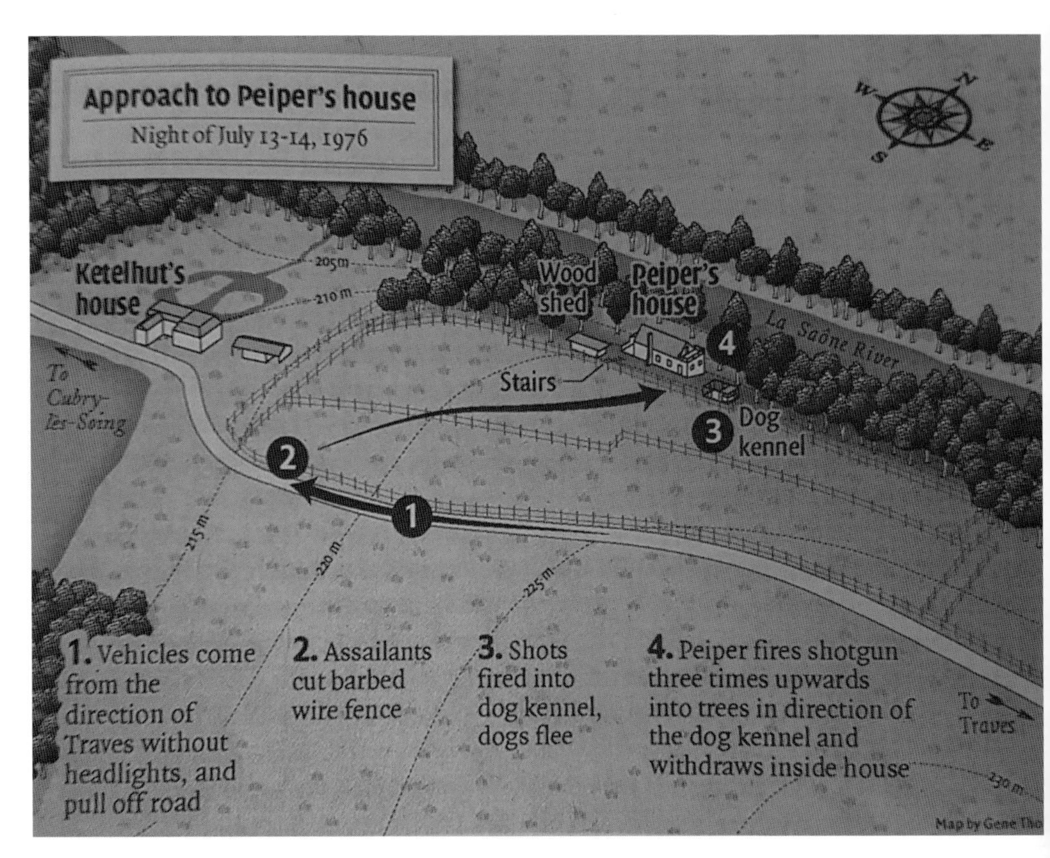

A map of Peiper's home and the surrounding area in Traves, France, where he died in 1976.

Joachim Peiper with Himmler and Sepp Dietrich in Metz, France, in September 1940.

A young Joachim Peiper.

Peiper sat 3rd from left in the front row at his Dachau trial in May 1946.

Peiper with Fritz Kosmehl and his wife Sigurd, Stuttgart, 1960.

Peiper being interviewed at his home in Traves, France, July 1976.

Ring that was given to SS members.

Peiper in SS uniform (Bundersarchive)

Joachim Peiper post war, possibly around 1960.

Peiper (left) with his father Waldemar and his elder brother Horst, taken early in the war.

Joachim Peiper during the Battle of the Bulge wearing winter clothing.

Peiper on trial at Dachau concentration camp, May 1946.

Peiper (left) and a colleague (date and location unknown).

Peiper at an official fucntion, whilst holding the rank of Obersturmfuhrer, to which he was promoted on 30 January 1939.

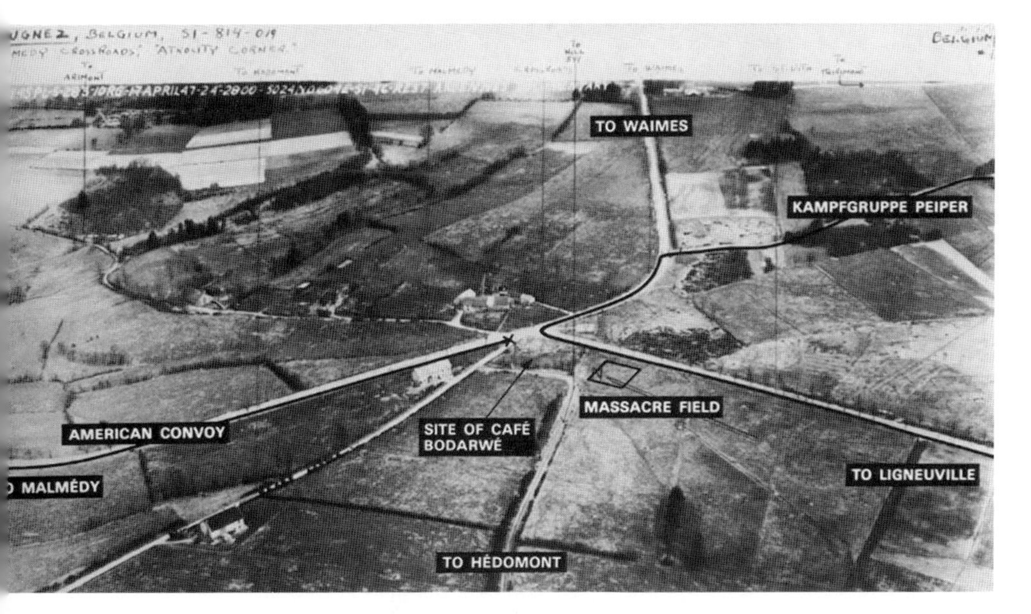

Overview of site of the Malmedy massacre.

The building at Dachau concentration camp where the trial was held.

American dead at Malmedy.

Uncovered dead bodies in the snow at Malmedy.

Kampfgruppe-Peiper during the Battle of the Bulge.

Six American survivors of the Malmedy massacre.

Memorial to the men who were victims of the Wereth massacre, December 1940.

Peiper's name being painted out of the road at Traves, France.

reconnaissance battalion under the command of Gustav Knittel, back to Stavelot to clear out the Americans, and reopen the supply lines.

Knittel and his men attacked Stavelot from the west on 19 December, but the Americans held firm and the Germans failed in their attempts at reopening the supply lines. It was while preparing for the attack on Stabelot that a large number of Belgian civilians were murdered by Knittel and his men.

The prosecution informed the court that they would provide evidence to show that throughout the early days of the operation, men of the 1st SS Panzer Regiment killed unarmed and defenceless prisoners of war and unnamed Allied civilians, not only at the crossroads south of Malmedy, where seventy-one bodies were discovered and where they attempted to murder a further forty-three who managed to escape, but at six other locations.

At Honsfeld it is alleged that in six separate incidents they murdered between twenty-eight and forty American prisoners of war.

At Buellingen, SS soldiers murdered between sixty-two and ninety American prisoners of war, and at least nine Belgian civilians in thirteen separate incidents.

In Ligneuville, between forty-eight and fifty-eight unarmed American prisoners of war were murdered in two separate incidents.

In twenty-one separate incidents in and around the vicinity of Stavelot, SS personnel murdered eight American prisoners of war and at least seventy-three Belgian civilians.

At Wanne, at least six Belgian civilians were murdered by SS soldiers during three separate incidents.

At Lutre Bois, an innocent Belgian civilian was murdered.

At Cheneux, between forty-one and fifty-one unarmed American prisoners of war were murdered by members of the SS during two separate incidents.

During two incidents at Trois-Ponts, four Belgian civilians were murdered by the SS.

At Stoumont, between 104 and 109 American prisoners of war were murdered by elements of the SS, over the course of a staggering twenty-four separate occasions, along with one Belgian civilian.

The SS murdered between 175 and 311 American prisoners of war, on 18 separate occasions at La Gleize, along with three Belgian civilians.

And finally, an American soldier who was starving and extremely cold, and who had been hiding in the woods for more than two weeks, decided that he had no option but to surrender. When he did, he was murdered by the SS on the order of the regimental commander and regimental surgeon.

This meant there had been ninety-four known incidents where members of the 1st SS Panzer Regiment had murdered between 538 and 749 American prisoners of war, and more than ninety innocent Belgian civilians. The prosecution believed these figures were only representative of the number of incidents which had actually taken place, and of those who had been murdered, but they had only quoted incidents for which they were happy they could provide evidence.

It was certainly going to be a difficult task for the prosecution to present their case in a wholly chronological fashion, as the murders had taken place during a fast-moving and changing battle. Much of the evidence that would be presented was in the way of statements taken from the defendants themselves, a number of whom had been involved in more than one of the incidents. There were occasions where some of the witnesses giving evidence against the defendants had previously been one of their comrades, alongside whom they had fought in battle.

After the war all captured members of the 1st SS Panzer Regiment were placed in the War Crimes Enclosure, Internment Camp No. 78, at Zuffenhausen. In total there were 993 of them. Most of the prisoners would have been under no doubt as to why they had all been detained together and not with men from other units or regiments. If anyone had not realised the seriousness of the situation they were in, it would not have been long before they worked out what was going on.

Once these men were interviewed and interrogated, they returned to their barrack block and informed their colleagues what had been asked of them, making the situation abundantly clear to one and all.

Fortunately for the officers and men of the 1st SS Panzer Regiments, 1st Battalion, their commander, Werner Herman Gustav Poetschke, who ironically was Belgian by birth, was dead. After the fighting in and around Malmedy in December 1944, the Division had been moved to Hungary. On 23 March 1945 while in attendance at a commanders' meeting south of Veszprem, he was wounded during an Allied mortar attack on their location, where he sustained serious wounds to his lower extremities. He died of his wounds the following day.

Poetschke's death provided an immediate, if not somewhat obvious, excuse for all members of the SS being held at Zuffenhausen. All they had to say was that they had acted under the direct orders, or 'superior orders', given to them by Poetschke. From a prosecution perspective there is the obvious retort, that an order to carry out an act that would constitute an obvious criminal offence, was not, and could not be, a lawful order. Any reasonably experienced defence lawyer would no doubt advise their client to claim that at the time of carrying out such an alleged act, they were acting under duress, in that they feared if they did not do as they were being told, they would have been killed themselves.

The American interrogators quickly realised that if they were to have a chance of getting any of their SS prisoners to begin talking to them, they would need to place them in to individual isolation, so that once an individual had been interrogated, he could not then inform his colleagues what he had been asked, and maybe more importantly, what he had said in reply.

To try and achieve this, on 1 December 1945 the top 500 prisoners of most interest to their American captors were moved to Internment Camp No. 2, Schwäbisch Hall, which by then was nearly 100 years old and had been a civilian prison before the war. Once there, the men were no longer kept in barrack-room accommodation, but rather in individual cells and the conditions under which they were held became more secure. None of them knew which of their former comrades they were now being held with. They were not allowed to communicate with each other and when taken out of their cells for interrogation were blindfolded by means of having a hood placed over their heads so that not only could they not see anything, but none of the other prisoners could identify them.

Between their arrival at the Schwäbisch Hall internment camp and late April 1946, when they were moved to Dachau, the original 500 German prisoners of war were joined by an additional 300, who were kept under the same strict conditions. Despite many of the SS prisoners being young men, either in their late teens or early twenties, it took months of interrogations before they even began to open up and begin talking about the events in which they had been involved. This was no mean feat because in essence, all these men being interrogated for information were also suspects in the same events.

It does us well to remember that these men were not just regular German soldiers, they were members of the SS. They were devout and committed Nazis who saw themselves as loyal and honourable individuals, committed to the Nazi cause and ideals. To agree to be a witness against one of their comrades would have been an alien concept to them.

Besides being members of the SS, they were also suspects in a number of events that resulted in the deaths of hundreds of American prisoners of war and innocent Belgian civilians. The order they were given at the outset of the operation when they were still at Blankenheim was that if captured, they should not give Allied forces any information about the murders in which they had been involved or witnessed.

For the American interrogators, the task of getting these men to talk was never going to be easy, as they found themselves up against a wall of silence preventing them from getting to the truth of exactly what these men had done.

After the prosecution had made their opening speech, a member of the defence team addressed the court (the prosecution had objected, but were overruled by the president of the court). In essence, the defence team asked that the court members and president not only kept an open mind on proceedings, but also ensure the defendants received a fair trial; they asked the court to set aside any personal feelings they might have about the charges against these individuals, which involved the alleged murders of fellow Americans. To ensure that the proceedings produced a fair trial, any thoughts that individuals of the court might have about revenge, or victors 'lauding it' over the 'vanquished', could not exist.

In closing, the defence counsel made the following statement:

> May the proceedings of this trial rise above any spirit of victor over vanquished as well as any popular passion or frenzy to retaliate for our fallen comrades. Let it be said at the conclusion of this trial that the mighty Army of the United States, even in the afterglow of victory and during our enemy occupation, have not destroyed the right of the fair trial which further demonstrates our spirit of democracy. The Defence counsels recognize that the Court itself is in a similar position to ourselves, but we have full confidence that each of you will abandon during this trial any spirit motivated by prejudice, hatred, or vengeance and will assume a dispassionate attitude.

The defence also added what I believe to be a somewhat incorrect statement in defence of what had taken place, by stating that the case was different from one relating to a concentration camp in that it was not a premeditated plan of murderous extermination carried out over a long period of years, but merely a case of the 'heat of battle', conducted by a desperate and nearly defeated enemy.

If the words, 'carried out over a long period of years', were removed from that statement, then this was most definitely a case of a premeditated plan of murderous extermination, and it most definitely was not correct to mention it in the same category as an act which had been carried out in the heat of battle.

The first witness called by the prosecution was 1st Lieutenant William R. Perl, who introduced himself to the court as being a member of the War

Crimes Branch of the United States Army, and the chief interrogator in what had become known as the 'Malmedy Massacre' case. Perl began answering questions concerning Josef 'Sepp' Dietrich, who had been a colonel in the SS. At the time of the Battle of the Bulge he was the commander of the 6th Panzer Army, and the man to whom Joachim Peiper ultimately answered.

Perl was asked if he knew who the guards were at the Internment Camp No.2 at Schwäbisch Hall. He replied that men from different units undertook that particular role, which he said in the beginning were American soldiers from a tank buster unit and a field artillery unit, but that the last men to undertake the role of prison guards at the camp were Polish soldiers; he didn't know what unit they were from.

In relation to Dietrich, Perl was asked if he had mistreated him or ordered others to do so. He replied in the negative to both questions. He was then asked if he knew if any of the Polish guards had mistreated Dietrich, to which he replied that he was aware Dietrich had been kicked by some of the Polish guards, and that he knew this as the defendant had told him about it, but that he hadn't wanted Perl to do anything about it. It appeared to have been of a minor nature.

As might have been expected once there was mention of a statement having been made, the defence stated that they intended challenging such confessions, inferring that they may have well been obtained under duress. This seems to be a strange statement for the defence to make, as at the time they were not aware of the content of any of the statements, so they had no way of knowing if they contained anything that was in the least bit contentious. The most sensible and professional manner in which to have dealt with the matter would have been to listen to the evidence against each of the men, and then decide if there was anything to challenge, rather than make a pre-emptive and collective statement which related to all of the defendants. It appears that one of their tactics was to challenge and question all of the statements and admissions made by any and all of their clients.

After a lengthy discussion, which at times was a borderline argument, the prosecution was finally allowed to read out the statement which Dietrich made to Lieutenant Perl on 28 March 1946, at Schwäbisch Hall.

The statement consisted of just seven paragraphs and besides providing minimal information about himself concerning his rank and command, it named two other men. The first was General Lieutenant Priess, the commander of the 1st SS Panzer Corps. This was a reference to Herman August Fredrich Priess, who at the end of the Dachau trial was found guilty of the murder of more than 300 Allied prisoners of war and 100 Belgian civilians. He was sentenced to twenty years imprisonment but was released from Landsberg Prison in October 1954.

The other person he mentioned was Joachim Peiper: 'The 1st SS Panzer Regiment as well as the combat group mentioned which was commanded by Standartenführer Joachim PEIPER during the EIFEL offensive 1944 to 1945 belonged to the Leibstandarte Adolf Hitler and therewith to the 1st Panzer Korps.'

The second from last paragraph of the statement read: 'I have made this statement voluntarily and out of my own free will, uninfluenced by duress, threats or harsh treatment.'

Two things struck me about this statement. First, he could have spoken about many events in which he had been involved during the course of the war; he could have spoken about his promotions or the medals he had been awarded throughout his military career, a statement that would have gone on for a number of pages, and no doubt taken several hours in its compilation. But instead he makes a statement which consisted of seven paragraphs and took up only three quarters of a page in size.

It seems highly unlikely that Dietrich sat down at a table and wrote or dictated such a statement without being prompted in some way. His statement was in response to his being asked specific questions.

Regardless of whether or not Dietrich realised it, by signing this statement he confirmed the link between Priess and Peiper and their respective units, which were known to have been in the immediate area of Malmedy in December 1944. A statement such as this is ultimately a link in the chain of evidence that is needed to convict somebody at court.

Second, the last two paragraphs of the statement are not verse that anybody would naturally come out with.

> I have made this statement voluntarily and out of my own free will, uninfluenced by duress, threats or harsh treatment. I swear before God that the facts in this statement are true and I am prepared to repeat them before any court.

They are the words of the person taking the statement so as to provide it with some credibility and to prevent any adverse suggestion about how it was obtained.

I was a police officer for thirty years and during that time I interviewed and took statements from a number of people for a plethora of different reasons. Whether it was an interview of a suspect or a statement from a witness, the only reason behind either was to gain evidence that would form part of a prosecution case in any subsequent criminal trial.

Most statements I ever took or wrote would always have a 'rider' at the end of them, saying something like:

'I have made this statement of my own free will, and am prepared to attend court if so required.'

On 14 April 1946, just over two weeks later, Dietrich made a further brief statement in which he identified two photographs as being that of Joachim Peiper. He probably did not realise he was in fact greatly hindering Peiper's own case.

This is the most damning of his statements and I believe it shows a realisation on Dietrich's part of the dire situation he was actually in. It was a case of loyalty to the SS against self-preservation, and the latter most clearly won the day.

This is what he had to say:

> During the EIFEL Offensive in December 1944 and January 1945, I was Supreme Commander of the 6th Panzer Army.
>
> On 12 December 1944, a conference with the Führer took place at Bad Nauheim. All officers up from Divisional Commander belonging to those units which were to be committed in the impending ARDENNES Offensive, participated in this conference. The Führer gave a three hour address at this conference. In this, he said among other things, that the impending battle must be won at all means. The decisive hour of the German people had arrived and it was to be or not to be. We would have to fight hard and recklessly. The Führer said furthermore that we would have to act with brutality and show no humane inhibitions. The Führer also said that a wave of fright and terror should precede us and that the enemy's resistance is to be broken by terror.
>
> In the order which I issued for the 6th Panzer Army for the EIFEL Offensive, due to the talk of the Führer, I ordered that our troops have to be preceded by a wave of terror and fright and no humane inhibitions should be shown.
>
> I can no longer remember the exact wording but this was the sense of the order. I ordered further that every resistance is to be broken by terror. However, I certainly did not order that the prisoners of war should be shot. I didn't mention prisoners of war at all. Whoever claims anything of the sort is speaking the untruth.

The last paragraph of the statement mentioned that it was made voluntarily and had not been influenced by threat, force, promise or duress. If ever there was a statement which did not require such an ending it was this one. Here was a man who had come to realise that he was facing the biggest battle in which he had ever been involved. The one to save his own life.

If ever there was an example of what is referred to as the witting and unwitting testimony sitting next to each other in the same statement, this was it. Dietrich was clearly and unequivocally stating that the order he had given to his men did not mention, nor had it ever been his intention for it to include, the killing of prisoners of war. Unwittingly, Deitrich was stating that whichever of his subordinates had given an order to kill Allied prisoners of war and civilians, had done so of their own volition and had not been done at his behest or suggestion. Although he had not named them, it was also as clear a reference to Priess and Peiper as it was possible to make without actually naming them.

The prosecution then asked Lieutenant Perl if he had ever interrogated Joachim Peiper, to which he replied, 'Yes'. He was then asked if he could see the man whom he knew to be Peiper in the court. Once again he replied, 'Yes'. He was then asked what number the man was wearing, to which he replied, '42'. Perl was asked if during his interrogation of Peiper the man had made a statement. He replied that he had. Perl was then asked a number of questions, exactly the same ones which had been posed in relation to the interrogation of Dietrich and the statements obtained from him.

The statement which Joachim Peiper had given to Lieutenant Perl on 28 March 1946, was then read out to the court. Like Dietrich's statement, there were elements of it which simply don't add up.

> During the EIFEL offensive in December 1944 and January 1945, I was commander of the 1st SS Panzer Regiment, L.SS.A.H. as well as leader of the Armoured group which was under my command.
>
> At that time my Armoured Group belonged to the Leibstandarte Adolf Hitler. The official name of the L.SS.A.H. was the 1st SS Panzer Division L.SS.A.H. The commander of the 1st SS Panzer Division L.SS.A.H. was at that time SS-Oberführer Willibald MOHNKE.
>
> The 1st SS Panzer Korps belonged at that time to the 6th Panzer Army which was under the command of SS-Oberst-gruppenführer and Generaloberst Sepp (Josef) DIETRICH.

The 6th Army was generally called by us 6th SS Panzer Army. However, I believe that the name 6th SS Panzer Army was only later adopted officially.

After the prosecution had finished asking Lieutenant Perl questions about his interrogation of Peiper, he then had to answer further questions from one of the defence team, namely Dr Leer, who was Joachim Peiper's representative.

Question: Could you tell the Court what you said before the first interrogation to Col. Peiper, before the start of the first interrogation, what you told Col. Peiper?

Answer: Yes. When he came in I told him: 'I saw you once before, in November or December, and I told you then it would be the best to tell me the full truth right now. You then told me that you don't know anything about these incidents. Due to this, we continued our investigation and found out about many killings in whole detail. You are in now for the second interrogation, after we interrogated almost all the others. Don't you want to tell the full truth now? You see, the more we go in to the case, the more we find out the full truth, and we know almost, maybe, everything already.' I then presented him with some of the statements, which showed that we already had quite some detailed knowledge of the happenings, and I told him that, as an officer, he must know that in his condition, it is the best thing to surrender unconditionally; that he should not repeat the mistake Germany made when she did not surrender one year before; that there was no sense to continue a hopeless fight. He then admitted the orders, everything pertaining to the orders, as read in the statement here. Of course, what I said are not the exact words of the conversation, but it is the exact meaning.

It is interesting to note that Dr Leer chose not to interrupt Lieutenant Perl at all. He just let him talk for as long as he wanted to, maybe in the hope that he was going to say something which might have contradicted what he had said when he was questioned by the prosecution. But rest assured Dr Leer would have remembered everything that Perl had said for future reference.

Question: Is it correct that you said that he had a life behind him which is now broken after the defeat of Germany? That his

> life from now on would be senseless because in a few days the SS organisations would be condemned in Nuremberg, and that now he had the opportunity to save the lives of his soldiers?

At this stage the prosecution objected to the defence's questions being put to Perl, because what they were asking him related to a statement which had not yet been introduced in evidence, but the court law member, Colonel Abraham H. Rosenfeld, somewhat surprisingly overruled the prosecution's objection, and instructed Lieutenant Perl to answer the question put to him.

> **Answer**: I remember that I once talked to Peiper about his future life having not much sense and not much hope under the present conditions. I believe it was in December, but it might have been in April. At this occasion I told him: 'You don't have much to expect from life any more, not with new events and developments. What remains for you is your honour as an officer and therefore you should speak the truth.' I mentioned his past, his glorious past, in order to make him speak the truth. I never told him that, by speaking the untruth or something similar, he could save any lives. Just the contrary. I insisted during all my interrogations, and at Peiper's interrogation too, that we don't want anything but the truth.
>
> **Question**: When were the statements of the other witnesses handed to Peiper, which you are referring to?
> **Answer**: In the course of the interrogation.
>
> **Question**: At the first interrogation at Zuffenhausen, or at Schwäbisch Hall?
> **Answer**: At his first interrogation at Schwäbisch.
>
> **Question**: Can the witness remember when that took place?
> **Answer**: Not exactly, but it must have been at the beginning of April.

Later the same day Lieutenant Perl was recalled to the stand by the prosecution to give further evidence in relation to his involvement, and further interrogation of Joachim Peiper. He was then asked questions in relation to another statement made by Peiper, the result of an interrogation which had been overseen by Perl.

> I, SS Standartenführer Joachim Peiper, make the following statement under oath, after first being duly sworn.

During the Eifel Offensive, in December 1944, I was SS-Obersturmführer and Commander in charge of the Armoured Group.

I myself was notified only very late about the particulars of the coming campaign, and I could not influence the preparation of this offensive.

About the 12th of December, 1944, in the vicinity of Kölln, a meeting with the Führer took place, at which all commanders, down to Divisional Commanders participated. I did not participate at this meeting. I do not know what orders were issued there, I only know that the Führer made a three hour address. Until the 10th December, I had not the slightest idea in which direction our offensive would take place.

On 14th December 1944, I was ordered to the Divisional Command Post, which was located in Blankenheim, where I had but a short conversation with the Division Commander, Oberführer MOHNKE. The field order and the other material, such as maps, disposition of the enemy, and so forth, I received from the 'Ia' of the Division, SS-Obersturmführer ZIEMSSEN. I did not read the material given to me at the Divisional Command Post, because I was in a hurry, and was also in a bad mood, because I disagreed with the entire preparation for the undertaking which looked highly defective to me.

I then returned on the same day to my Command Post, which was located in a Forester's house in the Blankenheim woods. First, I ordered my adjutant, Hauptsturmführer Hans Gruhle, to call a commanders meeting for the same day at about 1600 hours. This left me about two hours, which I used to study the material handed to me at the Division. The very first impression of the terrain which I got, with the aid of the maps, reassured my opinion that it was a desperate undertaking. I can remember that in this material, among other things, was an order of the 6th SS Panzer Army, with the contents that considering the desperate situation of the German people, a wave of terror and fright should precede our troops. Also, this order pointed out that the German soldier should in this offensive recall the innumerable German victims of the bombing terror. Furthermore it was stated in this order that the enemy resistance should be broken by terror. Also, I am nearly certain that in this order it was expressly stated that prisoners of war must be shot, where the local conditions should so require it.

Peiper was the first one of the defendants to admit part of the order which he had been given, and had originated from the meeting where Adolf Hitler had spoken for some three hours, had included the order to 'shoot prisoners of war where the local conditions of combat should require it', but he did not explain or comment on what the latter part of that actually meant. It certainly was a breakthrough moment in the investigation.

> This order was incorporated into the Regimental order, which was drawn up on my command by Hauptsturmführer GRUHLE, based on the material handed to us.
>
> Close to 1600 hours, the Commanders meeting took place at which the following persons participated: myself, Sturmbannführer Werner POETSCHKE, Sturmbannführer (then Hauptsturmführer) Josef DIEFENTHAL, Sturmbannführer Gustave KNITTEL, although he arrived a little late, Obersturmführer HARDIEK, Sturmbannführer Dr STICKEL, Hauptsturmführer OTTO, and I believe also the Major who commanded the Anti-Aircraft Battalion attached to me. In addition, Hauptsturmführer GRUHLE was at least temporarily present.
>
> At this meeting, I did not mention anything that prisoners of war should be shot when the local conditions of combat should so require it, because those present were all experienced officers to whom this was obvious.
>
> In the meantime, the Regimental orders were written and were picked up by the battalions, either during the night or on the following day.
>
> It is possible, although I don't know for sure, that the paragraph of the Regimental orders which dealt with the prisoners of war, and was taken from the Army order without receiving any additions, was not sent to the battalions in writing, but for reasons of security was only looked at in the Regiment, and remained there to avoid this order falling in to enemy hands.
>
> The above order, about which I have just talked, was signed by SS-Oberstgruppenführer and Generaloberst, Sepp DIETRICH.
>
> I know however that the order to use brutality was not given by Sepp DIETRICH out of his own initiative, but that he acted along the lines which the Führer had expressly laid down.
>
> When I was received on 14 December 1944 by Division Commander, Oberführer MOHNKE, he told me that he was present

at the meeting with the Führer and that on orders of the Führer, it had to be fought with special brutality. Whether on this occasion Oberführer MOHNKE used the word brutality, or something similar, I don't know any longer, at least that was the sense of it. Oberführer MOHNKE also said that the Führer stated, 'It has to be fought without humane inhibitions, and one should remember the victims of the bombing terror'. Oberführer MOHNKE also said on this occasion that the Führer spoke excellently for three full hours and that he had expressed the fullest confidence for victory. After the Führer's address, as Oberführer MOHNKE told me, only Field Marshall MODEL gave a 'Sieg Heil' to the Führer, nobody else spoke.

On the morning of 15th December 1944, I was at the Command Post of the 1st SS Panzer Corps, where the Commanding General SS Gruppenführer General Lieutenant PRIESS spoke in front of all Regimental Commanders and commanders of independent units under him. Independent units have at least the size of a battalion, but they are not under a regiment, but directly under a Division.

At this meeting about thirty commanders and leaders of independent units participated. Among others, I saw SKORZENY there for the first time. From my Panzer Group only Sturmbannführer Gustav KNITTEL was present, with the exception of myself. General Lieutenant PRIESS spoke about the meeting with the Führer and he also said that, on orders of the Führer to fight with reckless brutality. Here also, I don't know the exact wording, but I am nearly certain that General Lieutenant PRIESS used the words as they were in the Army order, when he talked about the manner in which to treat the enemy and fight him. Anyhow, out of his words emerged that we had to fight with brutality and that this was expressly desired by the Führer.

It is actually quite amazing that for the few months between December 1945 and March 1946, none of the SS men, regardless of whether they were officers or men from the enlisted ranks, said that much at all to their interrogators, but then all of a sudden from late February 1946, some of them had begun 'singing like canaries', and Peiper had actually admitted that an order did exist that instructed commanders to shoot prisoners of war if the circumstances warranted it.

One of the SS men on trial was Franz Sievers. His courtroom number was 59. He made an oral and written statement to Lieutenant Perl in the presence of Captain Schumacher. The interrogation which ultimately resulted in Sievers statement concerned the subject of whether he knew of the existence of orders to shoot American prisoners of war.

Before I look at the statement made by Sievers, dated 25 February 1946, it is worth noting a difference between the actual trial papers from which this statement is taken, and film footage that exists and is freely available on the internet. The written trial transcript records no courtroom discussion between Sievers and the prosecuting officer, Captain Raphael Schumacher, concerning the date which is shown on Sievers' statement, 25 February 1946, and the date on which Sievers claimed it was signed – some time in March 1946. The available video footage, however, clearly shows the discussion and disagreement taking place between Sievers and Schumacher concerning the date.

> On December 15 1944, I received in a forester's house or hunting castle, in the woods near BLANKENHEIM, at a Company Commander's meeting, the order, 'if it is necessary and the situation necessitates it, take no prisoners of war'. The Company Commanders of the 1st Battalion were present at this meeting, furthermore a Hauptsturmführer of the second company of the 501st Section Koenigstiger. Only I was present from my company.

The question here, is why had some of the defendants finally started to speak up and break what had previously been a really strong code of silence? There had been no admission previously from anybody about Hitler's order on killing prisoners of war, and all of a sudden, both Peiper and Sievers broke ranks and not only admitted its existence, but also admitted having received the order at a meeting where others, who had already denied knowing of such an order, had been in attendance.

After a recess in the late afternoon, the court reconvened for its final session of the day. Once again, First Lieutenant William Perl took the stand for the prosecution, where he was asked if he had interrogated one of the defendants named Arndt Fischer, to which he stated he had. The following statement was obtained from Fischer as a result of that interrogation and was read aloud by Perl:

> On the 20th February 1939 I volunteered for the SS Totenkopfverbände. From February 1939, until February 1940, I was in the concentration camp BUCHENWALD with an interruption of about 8 weeks

during which I was assigned to the concentration ORANIENBURG near Berlin. At the end of February 1940 I was transferred with Totenkopfverbände to the east.

Although at that time, there was no war with RUSSIA, yet we were in need of the east, that is in POLAND, as the population was not always friendly minded. From November 1940 until February 1943 I was continually in schools in the hinterland where I was first a pupil. From February 1941 on, I was a teacher in several SS schools. I lectured tactical subjects and Weltauschauung. Since June 1943, I belonged to the SS Panzer Regiment 1 'LSSAH'. During the EIFEL offensive from December 1944 until January 1945, I was adjutant of the 1st Battalion of the SS Panzer Regiment I 'LSSAH'.

If there were any doubts about whether an order was ever issued to shoot Allied prisoners of war, then Fischer's statement certainly clarified the matter. But once again the question had to be asked: why, after weeks of silence did he suddenly make such an admission? What was even more remarkable about Fischer's statement was that it named names.

On December 15, 1944, in a forester's house in BLANKENHEIM a written regimental order was handed to me by Hstuf. Hans GRUHLE, Adjutant of the SS Panzer Regiment I, 'LSSAH'.

In this Regimental order handed to me by Hstuf Hans GRUHLE, among other things it read that a wave of fear and terror was to precede our troops and that the resistance of the enemy was to be broken by terror. Furthermore it said in this regimental order that where the military situation should absolutely necessitate it, to shoot prisoners of war. After receiving the regimental order, without adding anything, I had this order copied anew, and changed the heading hereby from:

SS Pz Rgt. I. 'LSSAH'
to
I./(mixed) SS Pz Rgt I, 'LSSAH',

On the same day, another conference took place in the same forester's house at which Stubaf POETSCHKE, Commander of the I./(mixed) SS Pz Rgt I, 'LSSAH', also issued the same order to the company commanders. I also took part in this conference but I was not continuously in the room. However, at the time Stubaf

> POETSCHKE spoke about that we should not take any prisoners where the military situation absolutely required it, POETSCHKE also declared hereby that this order was a secret order.

It was fortunate for Fischer that he and his former SS colleagues were being held in separate cells and were guarded while being held at Dachau. In the eyes of his comrades, Fischer had committed the biggest crime of all by breaking the unwritten code of the Leibstandarte, whose motto was, 'My honour is my loyalty'. It is quite likely that some of his comrades would have murdered him for the disloyalty he displayed in naming them.

Regardless of the fact that today, such loyalty would be considered by many as misplaced, it was a loyalty that sustained these men through six years of bloody and brutal war.

The next piece of Fischer's statement, if one accepts it as being true, was just as damning for many of his other colleagues. Although he did not identify many of the men by name, by providing their rank and position within their unit, they were easily identifiable from official records.

> In my capacity as adjutant of the 1./(mixed) SS Pz Rgt. I, 'LSSAH' immediately after this conference, I had requested the officers who belonged to our battalion to sign the order which was retyped from the regimental order to battalion order described above.
>
> As far as I recall this signature was rendered on the reverse side of this described regimental order. The paragraph which I had written with the typewriter read approximately thus:
>
> 'Acknowledge order on reverse'.
>
> After the described conference I sat at a little table and called the officers to me for their signature before they left. I am pretty sure about it that I didn't also give the written orders along to the individual companies, which would bear the danger manifold that this order fell into the hands of the enemy and therewith would cause reprisals against German prisoners of war. More so a written forwarding of this order to every individual company would have cost more time and we were at that time in a hurry.

Fischer's fellow defendants listening to this statement being read out in the courtroom would have been shocked and mortified – and he would have been sat among them. He even went as far as to produce a sketch of the room and adjoining rooms in the forester's house in Blankenheim, where he had his colleagues sign a pledge, promising that they understood that the contents of the order were secret and should by no account be revealed to the enemy. The sketch was so detailed that it even included the table where he sat to have the pledges signed.

In his statement Fischer had mentioned the potential danger if a copy of this order were to fall into the hands of the Allies, purporting that it could lead to reprisals being carried out against German soldiers being held as prisoners of war by the Allies. Another interpretation of this could be that they didn't want a copy of such an order falling into enemy hands because, were they to lose the war, it could be used against them in any subsequent war crimes trial. The irony is that, to my knowledge, no copy of this order was ever discovered by the Allies, and its existence only came to light because of a verbal admission by members of the SS.

After reading out Fischer's statement, Perl was cross-examined by the defence lawyer, Dr Leer, who was representing Joachim Peiper.

> **Question**: Lieutenant, when did you talk over this statement of Colonel Peiper with Colonel Peiper, the statement of 21 March 1946?'
>
> [Before Lieutenant Perl could answer, the prosecution intervened.]
>
> May it please the Court, the Prosecution objects to further cross-examination on the statement of March 21, 1946 of Colonel Peiper, on the ground that he was previously cross-examined on this statement by the same counsel.
>
> **Dr Leer**: Might I say something to that? I was not able to say anything about that statement which was introduced by the Prosecution after the witness was recalled. The point of my question is merely for the sake of formal clarity with which I will later not be forced to delay the Court anymore. They are brief.
>
> **President**: The objection of the Prosecution is overruled.
>
> **Lieutenant Perl**: May I see the statement of the 21st of March? There are several statements taken on that day and I don't know which of the statements that is, by heart.

The statement to which Dr Leer was referring was in fact the prosecution's exhibit, number 11. It was pointed out to Dr Leer by the prosecution that it would be most helpful if when referring to a statement, he could quote an exhibit number rather than a date.

Lieutenant Perl: I discussed this statement with Peiper during the course of the interrogation, of course, and thus the other also shows several corrections. Maybe a week after the statement was taken, Peiper asked me whether he could have a copy of it or whether he could see the statement again. It was then in Wiesbaden for photocopying. As soon as I could get hold of the original again, I showed it to him, the original or a copy of it, but I didn't discuss it.

Dr Leer: My question asked for a briefer answer than that. When, Lieutenant, was this statement which you have in your hand discussed with Peiper?

Lieutenant Perl: Never after it was taken.

Dr Leer: Was it discussed and written down, all at the same time?

Lieutenant Perl: Yes.

Dr Leer: Without interruptions?

Lieutenant Perl: Certainly with interruptions of a few minutes.

Dr Leer: Another question, the records of which of the interrogations which you had taken down previously, did you put before Peiper before the proceedings in this interrogation?

Lieutenant Perl: I cannot remember it exactly anymore.

Dr Leer: Do you remember whether the accused Sepp Dietrich was interrogated by you prior to or after this interrogation of Peiper?

Lieutenant Perl: I believe Dietrich was interrogated afterwards.

Dr Leer: Is it possible that oral interrogations of the accused Dietrich happened prior to that time without these being reduced to writing?

Lieutenant Perl: When Dietrich was interrogated the first time he made his statement right then.

Dr Leer: Do you remember whether you put the record of the interrogation of Sepp Dietrich before the accused Peiper, either prior to, during or after the interrogation of Peiper?

Lieutenant Perl: I understand the question but it was almost on the same day and I cannot recall whom I interrogated first, Peiper or

Dietrich or whether I showed Peiper, Dietrich's statement. I believe that is what you mean.

Dr Leer: If the court will permit me one more question? Did you see the hoods which were passed around, from the inside?

Lieutenant Perl: No.

Dr Leer: I have no more questions.

Leer's cross-examination of Perl was certainly a strange one to say the least. Such questions usually have a purpose. They are asked in a specific sequence and build up to a 'killer' question at the end. By way of an example of how Leer's set of questions most definitely did not come into this category, I will highlight the question he asked about the hoods. Perl gave the one-word answer of 'No', and did not push the matter. It was so obscure a question in fact that the court's law member queried it.

Law Member: The Defence counsel's last question he said, 'Did you see the hoods which were passed around, from the inside', what did the counsel mean by the word 'inside' and by the question?

Dr Leer: It is claimed by some of the accused that the inside of the hood was dyed red. Now, since all of us don't know these hoods there might be several possibilities, which, as a lawyer, I am compelled to clarify to the extent which it is permitted by the Court. That might be blood….

Dr Leer's question seems somewhat at odds with the day's proceedings for two reasons. First, he only gave up his question when specifically asked by the court's law member, but didn't pose this same possibility to Perl when he was cross-examining him. Even though Perl answered 'no' to Dr Leer's question as to whether he had seen inside one of the hoods, he was never pushed on the matter. Questions in court cases are always asked for a reason; they are asked to prove a point and if they achieve what they are intended to, it can have a positive influence on a jury and a court. The obvious response for Dr Leer to make once Perl had stated he did not know the colour of the inside of the hoods, was to challenge the validity of this and assert that it seemed highly unlikely, given the number of defendants Perl had dealt with.

But it was an assertion he never made. He only brought it up when pushed on the matter by the court's legal member. He was, however, Peifer's lawyer, so he had every reason to find out every crumb of information he possibly could. Regardless of what Dr Leer was or wasn't trying to achieve, it brought an objection from the prosecution about the comment concerning the colour of the inside of the hood, an objection which was sustained by the court. The prosecution then questioned Lieutenant Perl again.

Prosecution: Can I ask you whether you saw the inside of any of the hoods in any colour other than the one that you have in your hand?

> **Lieutenant Perl**: Now looking at the inside, I remember that this is the color that the inside of the hoods had.
>
> **Prosecution**: What color is that?
>
> **Lieutenant Perl**: Yellow and white.
>
> **Prosecution**: How many of the hoods that were used at Schwäbisch Hall did you ever see?
>
> **Lieutenant Perl**: Maybe ten, I don't think we had any more.

On 27 May 1946, former SS 2nd Lieutenant Kurt Kramm took the stand to give evidence for the prosecution in the case of the Malmedy massacre. He sat in a chair with a 4-inch padded seat, designed to be used for long periods of time. It had been placed on a 3ft sq. raised stage in the centre of the room. Despite the fact Kramm could speak and understand English, he had an interpreter sat next to him in the shape of American soldier, Herbert Rosenstock. The man asking the questions was Lieutenant Colonel Burton F. Ellis.

Before Kramm entered the courtroom the president of the court, anticipating a possible volatile reaction, made the following announcement:

> I want the accused in the dock to make no display whatsoever and no demonstration of any sort, and to stop such conversation. I want no action of any kind when the witnesses come in to the room.

Kramm was asked some basic questions in relation to his name, rank and the unit he was a member of. He confirmed he was part of the staff of the 1st Section of the 1st SS Armoured Regiment LSSAH. The questions continued.

Prosecution: Did you take part in the Eifel Offensive of the German Army during the month of December 1944 and January 1946?

Kramm: Yes, sir, I did participate in it.

Prosecution: What was your assignment?

Kramm: I was the adjutant in the Headquarters Company of the 1st SS Armoured Regiment of the LSSAH.

Prosecution: Who commanded the 1st Battalion?

Kramm: SS Sturmbannführer, Major Werner Poetschke.

The fact Kramm was prepared to speak out against his former comrades was a major breakthrough for the American authorities, and a massive shock for the seventy-three defendants in the dock. No one was more surprised by Kramm's appearance and willingness to give evidence than Joachim Peiper, for whom loyalty was everything, and something he expected without question from those who served under him. The questions continued.

Prosecution: Are you familiar with any of the preparations made by the German Army for this offensive?

Kramm: Yes, I am.

Prosecution: What were the preparations that you are familiar with?

Kramm: Thorough training and lectures.

Prosecution: What were the lectures on?

Kramm: About the conducting of the war during the offensive to come.

Prosecution: Was there anything said in these lectures about the treatment to be accorded prisoners of war?

Kramm: Yes, there was.

Prosecution: What was said?

Kramm: The first statement I heard was in about the following words:

'It is to be hoped that everybody will know what to do in the action which will be performed. This humanity foolishness has stopped.'

Prosecution: Who made these statements?

Kramm: SS Sturmbannführer Werner Poetschke.

Prosecution: Did you attend any sand table exercises

prior to the commencement of the offensive?

Kramm: Yes, I did.

Prosecution: Who was present?

Kramm: All the officers of this 1st Section of the 1st Battalion and usually also all the non-commissioned officers of the rank of Technical Sergeant and above.

Prosecution: Did anybody speak at these sand table exercises?

Kramm: Yes.

Prosecution: Who was that?

Kramm: Major Werner Poetschke.

Prosecution: Did anyone else?

Kramm: Yes, the SS Lieutenant Colonel, Joachim Peiper.

Prosecution: What did Peiper say?

Kramm: We will fight in the same manner as we did in Russia in the action which will follow. The certain rules which would have applied in the West until now, will be omitted.

Prosecution: Did he say anything else?

Kramm: Speeches along the same general line. I don't remember the exact words.

By now the mood of the seventy-three SS defendants had changed from surprise to utter contempt and disgust. Their code of silence, and warped idea of honour, was being broken not only by one of their own, but an officer – a man who, in their eyes, should have known better.

Peiper considered the betrayal an outrage, and one committed by someone he had trusted and worked closely with during the latter years of the war.

Kramm continued answering questions about Peiper specifically, and what he had said and done about how he expected his men to conduct themselves in the offensive. In attempting to rally his men, Peiper reminded them of the

Allied air raids carried out upon German cities and the tens of thousands of German civilians who had been killed, in what those in Germany referred to as the terror raids.

With Kramm sat facing the judge and members of the General Military Government Court, or military tribunal, the five rows of defendants were sat immediately off to his left, and Peiper, wearing number 42 on a piece of white card around his neck, was sat in the front row, fourth from the left between Hermann August Friedrich Priess and Friedrich Christ.

Kramm identified Peiper in person and confirmed that at the time of the Ardennes Offensive he was the commanding officer of the 1st SS Armoured Regiment LSSAH. He added that after hearing both Poetschke and Peiper speak, it was clear in his mind that there was no need to accept any prisoners of war in any future actions.

Kramm confirmed that on 15 December 1945, while in the command post of the 1st SS Regiment, located in the woods near Blankenheim, he had seen a regimental order signed by Joachim Peiper, and which had been passed on to battalion level by the Regimental Executive Officer, Captain Hans Gruhle. The order contained such information as the route they would take, the march formation, and the sentence, 'The attack will be performed without regard for losses of our own and without mildness towards the enemy.'

While he was at the command post a meeting took place of the company commanders of the 1st Section, 1st Armoured Battalion, LSSAH.

Kramm identified those present as being 1st Lieutenant Fritz Christ, for the 2nd Company; 2nd Lieutenant Hans Steigler, the 1st Platoon leader of the 6th Company; Captain Osker Klingelhoefer for the 7th Company; 2nd Lieutenant Hans Bucheim was there representing the Battalion Headquarters Company; for the Forward Platoon, 1st Lieutenant Werner Sternebeck; and for the Headquarters Company, the Executive Officer, Untersturmführer Fischer.

Beoni Junker, who was the Commander of the 6th Company, was also in attendance but arrived after the meeting had already begun.

Having mentioned their names, Kramm then identified them individually to the court when asked to do so by the prosecution.

As part of the questions proffered by the prosecution, Kramm confirmed that Untersturmführer Fischer, who was one of those who had been at the meeting, had handed him a piece of paper which, in essence, was a certifying document. Kramm had to sign it to certify he would remain silent about its existence, and pass on its contents only to those who needed to know about it to perform their duties, which meant the men who served under their command.

By now there was absolutely no doubt that an order had been issued which had almost certainly originated from the conference at which Hitler had spoken. It was also clear that same order had reached the officers and men of the 1st SS Armoured Regiment. What the prosecution now wanted to establish, beyond all reasonable doubt, was the part that Peiper had played in the distribution of the contents of that order, and who exactly was responsible for carrying out the murders of the American prisoners of war and the Belgian civilians.

The business of the court finished at just after 5pm and reconvened the following morning at 8.30am. Once again the man giving evidence was Kurt Kramm. The day began with the prosecution clarifying a point over the meetings which had taken place, to ensure there was absolutely no confusion.

> **Prosecution**: Again, with reference to your testimony at the close of yesterday's session when you were speaking about the meetings that were held by the various company commanders, do you know what subjects were discussed and what type of speeches were made?
>
> **Kramm**: No. I was not present when the company commanders had their conference.
>
> **Prosecution**: Do you know what subjects were covered at the meetings?
>
> **Kramm**: Yes.
>
> **Prosecution**: What were the subjects?
>
> **Kramm**: The coming offensive with the tactical consequences and all matters which concerned the warfare and also the treatment of prisoners. That was the decisive conference before the attack.
>
> **Prosecution**: Are you speaking about the meetings held at the regimental command post or the company meetings held by the individual company commanders?
>
> **Kramm**: No. I am talking about the conferences which took place in the position of the 1st SS Armoured Regiment which took place in the forest of Blankenheim, in which the company commanders of the 1st SS Armoured Battalions were informed.
>
> **Prosecution**: I am referring to the meetings held by the company commanders, what kind of speeches did they make at these meetings?
>
> **Kramm**: At this conference a speech was made by the commandant of the 1st SS Armoured Battalion.

Even though Kramm spoke and understood English, the prosecution wanted to ensure there was absolutely no confusion about the specific meeting they were talking about, as this was extremely important to their case. Thus far, Kramm had been answering all questions in German. His answers were then translated to English by an English interpreter.

The prosecution asked Kramm to answer a number of questions in English, which brought an objection from the defence who pointed out that as Kramm had not been present at a particular conference he could not possibly answer any questions about it in either English or German. Their objection was overruled by the court, mainly because the rules of evidence which appertained in that particular type of court allowed witnesses to testify to hearsay evidence.

The court reporter then re-read the previous question back to Kramm.

> **Kramm**: I can only tell that I know that in this company meeting we had delivered speeches about the coming offensive and about all things which concerned the offensive.
>
> **Prosecution**: I believe that there was a mistake in the translation again. I am referring not to the regimental meeting but to the various company meetings that were held. Do you understand that or is that wrong again?
>
> **Kramm**: Yes. I understand it quite well.
>
> **Prosecution**: Will you translate it in English and we will see what you understand?
>
> **Kramm**: The company meetings were held after the meetings of the company commanders in the command point in Blankenheim campaigns.
>
> **Prosecution**: Do you know what kind of speeches the company commanders made at those meetings?
>
> **Kramm**: I know that the company commanders did deliver the news which they got in the meeting of the company commanders in the command point to the companies.

Kramm was then asked if he could identify another of the defendants, Kurt Sickel, who was the regimental surgeon of the 1st SS Panzer Regiment, which he could and did.

The questions then changed very subtly to that of Joachim Peiper and the combat group under his command. Regardless of what Peiper was thinking and how he was feeling about the events that were unfolding before his eyes, he gave nothing away. He would have made a fine poker player, sitting visible to one and all in the front row of defendants; any inner rage and anger he may have been experiencing, he kept well hidden. It is hard to believe, considering him in a purely physical sense, that here was a man charged with mass murder. He wasn't particularly tall, neither was he physically imposing, and with his short, neatly cut, tidy looking, swept back black hair, he could have easily been mistaken for a teacher, bank cashier, or even a lawyer.

The prosecution then continued with its questioning.

> **Prosecution**: Do you know the route of march of the Combat Group Peiper during the Eifel offensive?'
> [Kramm replied that he did. Everybody in the court would have then known exactly where this line of questioning was going. Once again Peiper showed not a flicker of emotion.]
>
> **Prosecution**: Do you know the approximate time of day that the point reached the various villages and also the time when the main body reached the same villages?
>
> **Kramm**: Yes. I know the time too.

Kramm was then asked by the prosecution to stand up and go look at a large map on the wall off to his right, and by using a pointer, trace the route taken by Combat Group Peiper during the Eifel offensive. Kramm begun by explaining that the group left Blankenheim at about two o'clock in the morning of 16 December 1944.

The following is in Kramm's actual words spoken in English, not from a translation. Some of what he says is not grammatically correct.

> **Kramm**: Then the armoured group were driving on Highway of Blankenheim to Dahlem. We were driving on the highway from Blankenheim to Dahlem and reached a point between the two locations, it is called Forsthaus Schmidtheim, about 8 o'clock am on December 16, 1944. Here we longer stopped. In the noon of December 16, 1944, the armoured troops were driving from Forsthaus Schmidtheim over Dahlem, over Stadkyll, over Kronenburg, over Halllschlag to Losheim. Losheim was reached by the point about 7 o'clock pm. We needed the night to drive from Losheim to Lanzerath. In the morning of December 17, 1945, we attacked for the 1st SS Panzer Regiment started.

Prosecution: Did you mean 1944?

Kramm: 1944, yes. Losheim was reached by the point, Honsfeld was reached by the point about 7 o'clock am, on December 17, 1944. The centre of the column reached it about 9am. From Honsfeld we attacked to Bullingen. Bullingen was reached by the point about 11am and by the centre, about 12 (noon). From Bullingen the armoured group left the highway and were driving on narrow roads over Shoppen to Thirimont. Thirimont was reached by the point about noon, the midst of the column reached it about 1230. From Thirimont the armoured group marched north in the direction of the highway from Waimes and Ligneuville.

Prosecution: Will you trace now on the map, the road that was followed by the Combat Group Peiper from Thirimont to Ligneuville?

Kramm stood up, walked over to the map, and slowly begun tracing the route as requested. While he did so, the prosecution continued with their questions.

Prosecution: Will you describe the route by directions?

Kramm: From Thirimont north direction on this road (indicating) to the highway from Waimes to the crossroads south of Malmedy.

Prosecution: When you reached the highway from Waimes to the crossroads south of Malmedy, which direction did you turn?

Kramm: We turned left and headed to the south.

Kramm continued with his detailed description of the route taken by Combat Group Peiper, the villages passed through and the times of their arrival. This included Beugnes which was reached by 2pm. From there they headed south towards Ligneuville, with the main body of the column not reaching there until roughly 3pm, some two hours after the head of the column had arrived. After leaving Ligneuville sometime shortly after 4pm, the column drove west, by which time it was already dark, and headed towards 'Lodnitz' (possibly Lodomez?), and from there on to the outskirts of Stavelot, where they arrived at about 10pm, although the bulk of the column didn't arrive until round about midnight, where they stayed for the rest of the night. The following morning after a few hours rest and sleep, the column attacked the village of Stavelot and had left there by 10am.

From Stavelot the next village, Trois-Ponts was reached at about 11am, where they turned north and headed towards La Gleize, where different elements of the column arrived between noon and 1.30pm. On leaving La Gleize the column headed west in the direction of Cheneux, where they arrived at 2.30pm.

Kramm confirmed that Combat Group Peiper had reached the village of Stoumont sometime on 19 December 1944, but he couldn't be certain at exactly what time, as he had been wounded the previous afternoon during fighting at the bridge between La Gleize and Cheneux.

What is incredible about Kramm's evidence is the detail it contained, taking into account his court appearance at Dachau was some seventeen months after the actual events had taken place, and there is no reference in the trial transcripts that he was reading from a statement he had made previously, or notes he had prepared. A good example of this was when he was asked if he knew the order in which the different elements of Combat Group Peiper had set off from Blankenheim on 16 December 1944:

> On the morning of December 16th, Combat Group Peiper took off in the following order: first the point platoon commanded by Obersturmführer Werner Sternebeck; then the 10th Panzer Grenadier Company commanded by Obersturmführer Georg Preuss, and elements of the 12th Panzer Grenadier Company with cannon SPWs; then the 1st SS Tank Company; then the 11th Panzer Grenadier Company; then the 6th Panzer Company; then the main part of the 9th Tank Engineer Company; then the 7th Tank Company commanded by Hauptsturmführer Oskar Klingelgoefer.
>
> **Prosecution**: Lieutenant Kramm, who commanded the 9th Panzer Pioneer Company?
>
> **Kramm**: the 9th Tank Pioneer Company was commanded by Obersturmführer Erich Rumph.
>
> **Prosecution**: Continue then with the order of march will you?
>
> **Kramm**: Yes sir. The main part of the Anti-Aircraft Company of the 1st SS Tank Regiment; then the 3rd Tank Engineer Company of the 1st SS Tank Engineer Battalion.
>
> **Prosecution**: Who commanded the 3rd Tank Engineer Battalion?

Kramm: The 3rd Tank Engineer Company was commanded by Obersturmführer Franz Sievers: then the 2nd Tank Company commanded by Obersturmführer Franz Christ; then the 13th Armoured Infantry Company of the 2nd SS Panzer Grenadier Regiment; then the Armoured Tank Battalion '501' with Royal Tigers and then the Anti-Aircraft Battalion from the Luftwaffe.

If recounting the order in which the different elements of Combat Group Peiper had set off from Blankenheim on 16 December wasn't impressive enough, Kramm was then asked by the prosecution if he knew the order in which the elements of Combat Group Peiper left Lanzerath, which he then proceeded to do.

Kramm further explained how, on the morning of 18 December, elements of the 6th and 7th Tank Companies and the 3rd Tank Engineer Company were sent on a mission to find another bridge crossing over the River Salm, and were gone for most of the day, not returning until late in the evening, by which time the Armoured Group had already moved on to La Gleize. Kramm even knew that they were up against the forces of the 80th American Infantry Division as well as those of the 30th American Infantry Division.

It was at La Gleize that Kramm was captured by the Americans on Christmas Day and interrogated by them that evening in an American field hospital in Velviers, Belgium, during which he did not answer all of the questions put to him honestly.

In German Kramm was a 'Kampfmittel Offizier' or Ordnance Officer, which was the same role carried out in the British or American Armies by an adjutant. By the time of the Malmedy massacre, Kramm had only been part of Peiper's regiment for less than two months, having joined in October 1944.

Kramm was then cross-examined by the defence who began by commenting on the fact that he had an 'admirable memory' in being able to remember the names of the German officers and the formations of their units. He was then asked if he had kept a diary during the offensive.

Kramm: Yes, sir. At first I wrote a diary, then at second, it was the last war action which I have made, and after this time I was captured and did not see any more action after this.

Defence: I see. And during the offensive you kept a diary from hour to hour?

Kramm: No, sir.

Defence: When did you make your entries?

Kramm: I only made the entries when important matters occurred and I had to make entries into the combat daily journal of the battalion.

Defence: Where is the diary now?

Kramm: I burned it before I was captured.

Defence: When were you captured?

Kram: Christmas Day, 1944.

Defence: And the entries which you made in your diary, referring to the events between December 16 and December 24 (1944), remain so vividly in your memory. Despite the fact that you burned this diary in December 1944?

Kram: Yes, sir.

It strikes me as strange that somebody would, or could, be able to remember such detailed information and recount it verbatim some seventeen months later.

Later the same day a statement from one of the defendants in the trial, and a man who had already been mentioned by a number of the witnesses, was read to the court by a member of the prosecution team. The defendant in question was Untersturmführer Hans Hennecke.

His statement told how he was requested to attend a previously mentioned conference which had taken place on 16 December 1944, at a forester's house at Schmidtheim, which had been taken over as the regimental command post. He had gone there in company with Obersturmführer Kremser. He mentioned the names of five other men, including Kramm, as individuals who were also at the same conference. There were other German officers also present, but he did not know their names.

While at the conference, Hennecke specifically remembered seeing Standartenführer Joachim Peiper sat behind a desk in one of the rooms, the same room that company commanders entered for their conference. Hennecke did not personally attend the conference. In fact, shortly before it began Kremser sent Hennecke back to the company, to assemble the platoon leaders and tank commanders, and to wait for him to return. Kremser returned from the conference and addressed his junior officers, a meeting at which Hennecke was also in attendance. He quoted Kremser as saying:

> I have just come from a conference with the Regimental Commander, and have instructions to refer you again to his order to drive on recklessly, to give no quarter and to take no prisoners. When you go back to your tanks, repeat Peiper's order to your men.

This was the second time that Kremser had given this order to his men, having done so the previous afternoon while in the forest at Blankenheim. As if to emphasise the points about 'giving no quarter', and 'no prisoners are to be taken', he reminded his men to think of their parents, brothers and sisters, and the Allied bombing raids on some of the towns and cities in which they lived.

The second from last paragraph of Hennecke's statement said the following.

> In our regiment, among all the officers, non-coms and men, the order which Obersturmführer Kremser gave us was not known as anything else but 'The order' of Standartenführer Peiper. It was always called 'Peiper's order', and this was well-known in the 1st SS Panzer Division LSSAH. Everybody knew that by that it was meant to shoot prisoners of war.
>
> After Kremser gave us this order, we returned to our crews. I went to the camp fire where the crew of Oberscharführer Skote and another crew were, and repeated the order given to us by Obersturmführer Kremser, which was the order about the shooting of prisoners of war.

The biggest unanswered question as far as I am concerned, is why the trial of these seventy-three former members of the SS did not include charges in relation to the eleven black soldiers who were also murdered on the same day at the village of Wereth, just fourteen miles away from Malmedy, and is known to have been carried out by members of the 1st Panzer Regiment LSSAH.

The atrocities carried out at Wereth were in many ways much worse than what happened at Malmedy, not in the number of men who were killed, but the brutality of the murders. Many of the 'Wereth 11', as they eventually became known, had their legs broken, fingers cut off and skulls caved in with what was believed to be rifle butts, the first two elements of which suggesting they were tortured before being eventually murdered.

There remain many unanswered questions about the events which took place at Malmedy and Wereth. Sadly, many of those who were responsible for the murders which took place there either escaped punishment altogether, or ultimately served such minimal sentences, it could be argued that justice was not served for the families of those who were murdered.

Chapter Eleven

Prosecution Witnesses

The following seven men were all members of the SS and were involved in the German offensive which included the Malmedy massacre. They gave evidence against their former comrades and, to differing degrees, all revealed details of the secret orders which included not taking any enemy prisoners. The question is why?

Sturmmann Horst Jaeger identified 2nd Lieutenant Hans Hennecke as one of those who had given the 'no prisoners' order.

Rottenführer Ernst Koehler was a gunner in a tank, and identified 2nd Lieutenant Hans Hennecke as the person who had given the order in relation to the taking of no prisoners.

Sturmmann Klaus Schneider was a tank radio operator.

Sergeant Kurt Plohman was a gunner.

These four men all served with the 1st Company, 1st Panzer Regiment LSSAH and identified 2nd Lieutenant Hans Hennecke as being the person who passed on the order in relation to taking no prisoners of war.

Sturmmann Hans Erich Licktmark served with the 2nd Company, 1st Panzer Regiment LSSAH, as an assistant clerk. He identified 1st Lieutenant Christ as the person who passed on the order that included the taking of no prisoners.

Sturmmann Hans Hubler served with the 2nd Company, 1st Battalion, 1st Regiment, 1st Division as a gunner. He identified 1st Lieutenant Christ (Defendant No. 7) as the person who had given the 'take no prisoners order' and Sturmann Mikolaschek (Defendant 37) who had taken boots from a murdered American prisoner of war.

There were no independent witnesses to the Malmedy massacre. The American prisoners of war who survived it and eventually made good their escape were limited in their ability to identify individual German officers or soldiers who had actually carried out the murders of their colleagues, and the evidence provided by the men named above was limited to rank, unit and the identification of those who had given the order to take no prisoners.

None of the prosecution's SS witnesses were asked if they could provide the names of anybody who had actually carried out the murders, the men who had pulled the triggers that fired the guns, which I would suggest would have been the obvious question to ask.

The way that the prosecution case was set up suggests to me that the Americans were not really interested in discovering who had carried out the actual murders, but rather that they were after the individuals who had given the orders which led to the murders being able to occur in the first place.

As I mentioned above, several members of the SS who were at Malmedy, and serving with units that were believed to have either been involved in the massacre or who were in the area at the time it took place, gave evidence for the prosecution against their fellow SS colleagues who they said had given the orders in relation to taking no prisoners. In doing so they also confirmed the instruction they had been given to keep quiet about the existence of that order. It makes no sense why they would have done that of their own free will. If they had all just kept quiet and said nothing, there is no way that the prosecution would have been able to prove anything against any individual. In fact the only evidence against them would have been that it was known from official German documents that the units these men had served with had been in Malmedy at the time of the massacre. In a court of law, that would not have been sufficient evidence to prove individual responsibility in the murders of any or all of the American soldiers.

This strongly suggests that these men were coerced in some way, either directly or indirectly, by threats being made against their families if they did not provide evidence against their comrades. There is also the possibility that they were made favourable promises if they provided such evidence.

Chapter Twelve

Letter from Landsberg

The following is a letter written by Peiper in October 1952, to an unnamed friend, from his cell in Landsberg Prison, or as the American's officially referred to it, 'War Criminal Prison No.1'. It is taken from the book by Patrick Agte, *Jochen Peiper: Kommandeur Panzerregiment Leibstandarte.*

This is an interesting letter, not only because it was written by Peiper, but because it was written seven years after the end of the war. Sufficient time, one would think, for him to have reflected on his life, especially the murders of American servicemen of which he was convicted at Dachau.

His words, in part, also provide an insight into what he felt about the offences of which he was convicted, how he views his life and the effect that the Second World War had on him.

> A war criminal sits on his folding bed in monastic solitude and day dreams. On the door it says 'Life Imprisonment' and on the calendar 'October 1952'. The stove sings, the spider looks for a new place to spend the winter, and autumn places its rough hand on the Swedish curtains. Thirteen years of separation from wife and family, five birthdays spent as a man condemned to death, and now this eighth Christmas in the penitentiary. A really great way to spend your youth. No animal should be this badly treated. Man is capable of great sacrifice and great vileness. Oh, how endlessly long must the chain of experience be before we even begin to sort it all out. The wartime generation has learned about others. And in Landsberg there is even more time to examine this knowledge and to try to make sense of it.

My immediate thought was that I was reading the beginning of a novel. It was as though he was writing about somebody else. An imaginary 'third person' who he felt sorry for because of the personal hardships he was having to endure. His most extraordinary comment is: 'No animal should be this badly treated. Man is capable of great sacrifice and great vileness.'

If the comments relate to how he felt he was being treated in Landsberg Prison, then he was borderline delusional, with little or no empathy for his fellow man – or rather those who were his victims.

> When we entered the world of barbed wire for the first time seven and a half years ago, we were like children who had lost their mother during the night. Growing up and maturing under the simple rules of the front lines, we found ourselves unable to grasp the new rules of the game. Whoever initially said that a policy blinded by anger would have its eyes opened by the truth, soon had to admit that you can expect very little justice when a blood-soaked figure needed to be painted on the wall for demagogic purposes. However, our good conscience was limitless and so was our ignorance. The state had only taught its youth how to use weapons.

Once again he appears to be distancing himself from the atrocities carried out by men under his order and command, instead blaming the German authorities, which I can only assume must be a reference to Adolf Hitler and the Nazi Party.

> We had never practised how to behave in the face of betrayal. Yesterday, we were still a part of the Wehrmacht; today, we are shunned and outlawed, whipping boys surrounded by a howling mob. We, who so far had only known a part of the impulse for self-preservation, courageous trembling in the face of danger, now had to get used to shouts of 'Stop, thief!' and to denunciations by those sorry figures who wished to rise by stooping low. Who could have kept from having doubts about Germany? Whose mouths weren't shut in disgust?

Here, Peiper appears to be quite shocked at what he sees as abandonment by the ranks of the Wehrmacht, the German Army. He seems somewhat surprised that men he saw as fellow countrymen could so easily and readily disown him and his comrades in the SS, because despite what he and his men had done, in his eyes, it had been done for the benefit of the German people.

> As our living space gradually constricted, from camp to barracks to cell, we became blind to what bound us together and could see clearly that which separated us. Distrust and spiritual nihilism took the

> place of comradeship. Everyone pointed out the failure of someone else and used accusation as an excuse for his own behaviour. 'Homo vulgaris' had freed himself from his chains. Primitive instinct celebrated its liberation from all restraint and we ourselves trampled about on others with self-destructive joy. Hunger swung its whip and human dignity cringed. Honourable tradition and proud class consciousness bowed to the ground for a cigarette butt. Was it any wonder that the vengeful enemy assault found many weak positions among us? Discord and distrust are poor advisors in the court room. Regardless, the mission could not have been accomplished. Those who had ensnared us had put too much work into their preparations. Knowing this, we entered the arena and stood silent for three long months in the pillory. For three times thirty days we were dragged through the gutter behind the victor's chariots.

His Germanic heritage meant that he demanded loyalty from his men, no matter what the cost to any of them individually. But to many of them, once the realisation kicked in that they were no longer in control of the events unfolding around them, events that were ultimately going to determine their own fate, self-preservation kicked in. He was shocked to find that some of his fellow SS colleagues were suddenly not so loyal to one another and were prepared to say and do anything necessary to save their own souls. Such conduct was totally alien to Peiper, who had been taught that pride, honour and tradition were what truly defined a man, and that to move away from what he saw as such basic principles was immoral to him, and certainly not how a man such as himself should or would conduct himself.

> The meaning of freedom is first learned by losing it. What a priceless gift this seems to those imprisoned. Only someone who has lost his freedom can dare to estimate how long a day can be and what it can mean when the nightmare of concern and uncertainty descends upon our next of kin for four years and seven months. Each of us was granted 23 cubic metres of breathing space. From then on, our entire being stood on tiptoe in our cells.

It is as though he expected some kind of luxurious incarceration while being kept as a prisoner, totally bereft of any grasp or understanding of the enormity of why he was actually there.

> Slowly things quieted down around us, except for the eternal rumble of our bellies and the song of life proclaimed by the blackbirds mornings and evenings. Oh you blackbirds! Is there any prisoner to whom you haven't given new hope?
>
> Nerves, raw from the prosecutor's lash, welcomed isolation. Our fists opened slowly and savage protest against fate faded. Only the lack of understanding remained, anguish for our loved ones and our quarrels with Providence, which had cheated us disgracefully of an honourable bullet. We learned how to sit in the twilight.

Peiper seems to believe that if given the death sentence, he and his cohorts were honourable men, and that as soldiers they were collectively entitled to be sent to their maker by a firing squad, meaning a bullet rather than the rope. There was, however, a major flaw with this belief, because neither Peiper nor any of his former colleagues merited any such entitlement, no matter how many battles they had fought in or medals they had been awarded. Peiper and his men, responsible for the murders of unarmed American prisoners of war and innocent civilians, were nothing more than cowards and common criminals who had willingly and happily taken the lives of other human beings simply because they could. That is not how an honourable person would even consider acting.

By carrying out the murders of so many people, Peiper was being disrespectful to the memories of the thousands of other soldiers who had been, or were, honourable men. A fact that he was unable to comprehend.

> The further we sank, the more the present faded, the nearer we came to our roots and, the more the past could be seen in a stronger light. The old battlefields became fields of renunciation and our fallen comrades the example and guardians of our conduct.
>
> The hard lesson began to dawn that life gave nothing without reason, that all of life's fortunes generally come with a price. Even the youngest among us never shirked in the face of the enemy.
>
> We sat in Germany's darkest corner and looked back at our sun-soaked flight of Icarus. No one should cast down his eyes. What did our inadequacies and mistakes count against our ardent hearts which we were ready to bring to bear anytime and anywhere? Supermen, men, and those less than men had crossed our path and it turned out that these categories were always fluid. The more we progressed and moved away from the clichés, the clearer it seemed that life, like light,

> consisted of complementary colours. Nothing was painted in black and white, but in shades of grey. Very slowly, things grew brighter again.
>
> We were young and challenges were inevitable. But who dies willingly on the gallows? We called out to Germany, and heard not an echo. We played chess through the walls, learned sign language and in an emotional manner wrote our obituaries.
>
> Then we became tired and indifferent and gave up our eavesdropping along with our hopes. We became unfair and bitter.
>
> Was there any decent guy who hadn't been jailed or any goodwill that hadn't been trampled? No matter, many of us rejected the human race, became misanthropes, and dedicated our brain and glandular activity henceforth only to the production of rancour. There is that type of person who can be recognized anywhere by an inexhaustible memory which cultivates old resentments. Me.

Peiper uses such words as *misanthrope* – a hater of humankind, and *rancour*, to describe how he was feeling because of his treatment by the Allied authorities, which he perceived to be unfair and unwarranted. But I believe the more relevant question is, how did he, as a convicted war criminal, honestly believe he would or should be treated? The reality is that, regardless of how some of his interrogators behaved, he was treated much better than he had treated his victims.

Having said all of this, it is clear from his writings that Peiper did not see himself in the same light. In his misguided mind, he was a loyal German soldier doing nothing more than his duty, and that which he had been ordered to do. As a member of the Waffen-SS he had played his part in trying to ensure a German victory. He believed he had conducted himself honourably in accordance with a code by which he and many others had sworn to abide. Now that the fighting was over and the war was lost, he felt betrayed and abandoned by elements within his own country, but more importantly by some of those with whom he had served and fought alongside, something he found difficult to reconcile with his own sense of loyalty.

Peiper had known nothing other than Nazi doctrine throughout his entire adult life. He had joined the Hitler youth when he was 18 years of age and joined the SS later that same year. His first commanding officer was Gustav Lombard, a staunch Nazi, an anti-Semite, and a man who went on to command the notorious SS Cavalry Brigade during the war; the brigade was responsible for the murders of tens of thousands of Jews throughout the Soviet Union.

By 1945, Peiper had been a member of the SS for nearly twelve years, the last six of which had been spent fighting a war. While many historians and readers will find Peiper's conduct and some of his actions incomprehensible, as far as he was concerned, he had merely been fighting a war in the only way he knew.

> Others recognized that the pseudo, democratic motto, 'Here we are all equal', was no more than stupid, empty words, a life preserver filled with lead and dragging you in the gutter. They fought with all their strength against the mass mentality and the continuous drag downwards. They became philosophers and attempted to preserve their internal freedom by conscious individualization and differentiation. They eventually sat in jail as if in an armchair. The most fortunate however, were those who knew how to make the best out of any situation and had the same outlook on life as a may-fly. Who hasn't run into these happy creatures whose native wit, even in the nastiest of situations, can't come up with an even nastier reply? We all began to lead withdrawn, introspective lives, put on masks, and bared our teeth. We all flapped our wings until they were sore and developed calluses which protected the elbows.
>
> When your life runs on behind stone walls, separate from wife and children, it is hard to remain just and objective. Young men pulled in powerless anger at their chains, felt their strength weaken and their courage tire. The levelling continued.
>
> The time was so hard, that we forgot it quickly, like a bad dream. It brought indolence and torment with it, spilled over its banks, and could no longer be exorcised by magic scratchings on the wall. We began to tell time by shaving days and pudding days.
>
> What got into our death-row cells from the outside wasn't calculated to make dying easier for us either. We discovered that we had belonged to a criminal organization and had served an unjust state. A slimy flood of investigative literature and memoirs produced explanations from diplomats and military men who had apparently worked for the defeat of their fatherland. We seemed to be a 'Decius Mus' fallen into a cesspool. Henceforth, there was no possibility of charting our position in the gloomy cellars of our ghostly country. The only fixed point in this chaos was the quiet heroism of our wives and mothers.

The more I read through the letter the more I came to understand that what I was reading were not so much the meaningful words of an intelligent man, but more the inane ramblings of a troubled mind, intent on justifying his existence by blaming his circumstances on others. The following sentence, I believe, evidences just how confusing he found life as a post-war, defeated German: 'We discovered that we had belonged to a criminal organization and had served an unjust state.'

It could be argued that Peiper was one of the tiny cogs that made up the giant wheel of Nazism, where the rules were whatever was laid down by the Führer, and something was only wrong if Hitler said it was. Peiper, therefore, could not see anything wrong in his actions or behaviours.

When such a state exists, the boundaries of 'normality' quickly become blurred and insanity becomes the new normal.

> But time not only separated, it also healed. Gradually and timidly, a national consciousness began to find a foothold outside. The fad for corpse looting was over. Order and long-suppressed, credible decency returned. And with these first skirmishers our comrades who had long held their tongues stepped back onto the scene. The pariahs of the post-war period had not forgotten their even less fortunate brothers. What did it matter that their readiness to help was inversely proportional to their previous rank? Germany's most loyal sons have usually come from small cottages. For us, however, it was as if a cut-off battle group had finally got air-dropped supplies, and, taking a deep breath, realized that it had not been written off. A Panzer radioman, blinded in the war, sat in some damp cellar apartment and wove a cushion cover for his condemned tank commander. A double amputee tore himself from his favourite book, and helping hands moved on distant continents. Shouldn't a weak spark of hope flare up again? A nonsensical period began to recover its meaning.
>
> We had become so defiant and surly because of continuous beating, that the alienation process was almost irreversible. Suddenly we felt again the revitalizing breath of fresh air of the comradeship borne of the front lines and became aware that there were other values on the outside besides rewarding the vulgar and showing contempt for all values. We gained a new understanding of the difficulties of life outside the gates, and the belief that Landsberg was the centre of the earth died.
>
> We found the concept of tolerance through pressure and ferment, and it may be that the value of those lost years lies in that tolerance. We first had to push into the region of self-understanding, so difficult to reach, before we found our human shortcomings.

And there, in this hard way, we began to learn to envy ourselves. Then in our fight for the truth and the essence of things, we first became conscious of the relativity and the subjectivity of any point of view. After a hard learning period, a broader outlook emerged from narrow-mindedness, and we threw off our blinders.

While the former senselessness of our period of suffering changed almost unnoticed into significance and understanding, a great change also took place on the outside, and the enormous sacrifices of our people received noticeable justification. Where would the torn-apart West be today, without each of those dikes of German bodies that were so important to history and that can no longer be ignored? The line of occidental combat outposts runs in a wide circle from the Caucasus to Finland. Representatives of our entire culture kept watch silently. And although their grave mounds are levelled and many nations are still ashamed of their noblest sons, it is still only thanks to this avant garde that Genghis Khan's heirs didn't ride their tanks all the way to the Atlantic.

Let us bury our hatred for their sakes, comrades. History will be a fairer judge than contemporaries blind by anger. The danger is so menacing and the need so great, that no one can be allowed to fail to answer the call.

Never forget that the first European fell in the ranks of the Waffen-SS, that those killed after the war mostly came from our ranks. It only became open season on them because of their belief in the indivisible unity of western society. Consider the evidence of their blood. Don't take half measures. The idea of Europe is the only political ideal that is still worth fighting for today. Never was its realization closer. Strangle lies, punch slander in the nose, help your neighbour and the war widow. When everyone goes back to simple values, gives up egoism, makes a virtue of poverty, and once more feels himself responsible to all, then once more we will get the carts out of the mud; the dams will be ready when the storm tide comes.

During the war our proud divisions were considered a solid elite.

According to captured documents, our steadiness made us a legend in every nation. Hopefully our children will be able to say the same of us, that in misfortune we too were not unequal to our fate, that we ourselves in the Diaspora provided the leaven for reconciliation and the European idea. I salute everyone Who Remained Free in Prison.

Chapter Thirteen

Peiper's Life After Release

In 1954, Peiper's already commuted sentence was further reduced from life imprisonment to a term of thirty-five years, but despite this he was released from Landsberg Prison, just two years later in December 1956.

Peiper was assisted in securing his release from incarceration by HIAG, an organisation founded by a group of former high ranking Waffen-SS men, in the newly formed West Germany, in 1951. The group's main objective was for the Waffen-SS to receive official recognition and be allowed to re-form in to a newer version of what it had once been, or, in its own words, 'to achieve legal, economical and historical rehabilitation of the Waffen-SS'.

To help achieve those goals, the HIAG utilised contacts with members of German political parties, while engaging in propaganda exercises aligned with the use of historical denialism. In other words, the falsification and distortion of historical facts. Understandably, the very existence of HIAG caused some controversy in a post-war West Germany where the wartime exploits of the SS and the Nazi Party still caused embarrassment.

After his release from Landsberg Prison, Peiper initially took up employment with the Porsche motor company based in Stuttgart – but life as a civilian did not run smoothly for him. Ferdinand Anton Ernest Porsche, more readily known by the name Ferry Porsche, had promised Peiper a senior management position, but his rise in the company came to an abrupt end when Italian workers accused him of being involved in, and responsible for, the Boves massacre, written about elsewhere in this book. The power of the trade unions came into force; they were unhappy that a convicted war criminal would hold such a lofty position within the company. The irony of this is that Ferry Porsche's father, Ferdinand Porsche Senior, had spent a period of twenty-two months in prison after the end of the war for his association with the Nazi Party. During the war he had designed and built military vehicles such as the Kubelwagen for them.

Because of the negative publicity surrounding Peiper, and his direct connection to the murder of American troops at Malmedy, sales of Porsche vehicles in the United States were badly affected, forcing the company to terminate his employment with them. This led to Peiper filing a lawsuit against Porsche, which resulted with him receiving compensation of six months wages.

Making the transition from being a member of the military, especially during a time of war, back to being a civilian, was never going to be easy. But add in the factors of having been on the losing side, as well as a member of the Nazi Party, then things were always going to be more demanding. Peiper had gone from the exalted position of high-ranking member of the SS, a man who was admired and respected by those who served under him and feared by others, to an ordinary member of the public. His position of power was now nothing more than a distant memory.

His behaviour became more calculated, by which I mean that he was careful about who he associated with publicly as he tried to make a new life for himself and his family in a post-war Germany. Luckily for him, his new world was to be found within the British, American and French sector of West Germany, rather than the Russian-controlled East Germany.

Privately, it was a totally different story. He maintained contact with a number of his ex-Waffen-SS colleagues, and played his part in assisting the work of the HIAG by down-playing some of the SS's controversial moments, while at the same time highlighting the reputation and positive achievements of its men and units.

In 1955, the Association of Knight's Cross Recipients (AKCR) was founded in Cologne by Alfred Keller, who had served as a General in the Luftwaffe during the war. He was a holder of both the Knight of the Order of Pour le Merite and the Knight's Cross of the Iron Cross.

Peiper, too, was a recipient of the Knight's Cross, following his actions during the Third Battle of Kharkov. On 10 October 1959, he attended the national meeting of the Association of Knight's Cross Recipients, or the Bearers of the Ritterkreuz, which certainly was a change in direction from his attempts at keeping a low profile. The meeting took place behind closed doors at Ratisbon, Germany.

The meeting was due to have closed with a speech by the German Minister of Defence, Franz Joseph Strauss, but he had to cancel late due to 'other duties', or perhaps he had second thoughts about how such a connection might have been viewed in a political sense. At the meeting, members of the association, who had come from across Germany and Austria, laid wreaths for the 2,000 recipients of the Knight's Cross who had been killed during the course of the war, out of an estimated 7,300 that had been awarded.

By November 2016, just twenty of those recipients were still alive, and at another secret meeting of the Association that year, only ten of them were able to attend the meeting, these included, Ludwig Bauer, Hugo Broch, Ernst Buntgens and Karl Konig.

Unlike the British system of military awards where a Victoria Cross is awarded for a single act of conspicuous gallantry, a Knight's Cross is only awarded after such acts had been carried out on three separate occasions. In essence, a man could not be awarded a Knight's Cross until after they had first won an Iron Cross Second Class, followed by an Iron Cross First Class for a second act of bravery.

On 13 August 1999, the then German Minister of Defence, Rudolf Scharping, took the decision to ban members of the Bundeswehr (German Army) from having contact with a member of the Association of Knight's Cross Recipients. His reason for doing this was because many of the Association's members 'shared neo-Nazi and revanchistic ideas which were not in conformity with the German constitution and Germany's post war policies'.

By the 1960s Germany had, to some extent, begun to recover financially from the war, and had an economy that was most definitely on the rise. Hand in hand with this came a change in the willingness to talk about and address the wartime atrocities carried out by members of the SS and the Nazi Party. This was brought to the fore by the Adolf Eichmann trial of 1961; Eichmann was found guilty of a total of fifteen counts, which included crimes against humanity; war crimes; crimes against Jews, Poles, Slovenes and Gypsies; being a member of the Gestapo, SS and SD, all of which had been designated as criminal organisations at the Nuremberg war crimes trials. Found guilty on 15 December 1961, Eichmann was sentenced to death by hanging, which was eventually carried out in the early hours of 1 June 1962, at Ramla Prison in Israel.

In considering the punishment Eichmann should receive, the court had concluded that he was a committed Nazi who believed in and agreed with their doctrines, and not just a minor individual who had simply been obeying orders from above.

This trial had been widely followed by the public in West Germany, and leading on from this there had been the Auschwitz trials in Frankfurt which had lasted for twenty months between 20 December 1963 to 19 August 1965.

Peiper found himself enveloped by part of the storm which had blown up around the new-found interest in West Germany, to prosecute some of those considered responsible for crimes committed during the war, who had not been dealt with at the post-war Nuremberg trials. Between 1962 and 1964, proceedings took place against Karl Wolff and Werner Grothmann, who, like Peiper, had both been adjutants to Heinrich Himmler. Unsurprisingly,

Peiper's name was mentioned and although he was not directly investigated or charged, just the mention of his name brought with it unwanted attention.

In 1964, Peiper faced accusations by the esteemed 'Nazi hunter' Simon Wiesenthal that he and his men were responsible for the arrest of Jews in Borgo San Dalmazzo, but the case was closed in 1969 without any charges having been brought against Peiper or any of his men.

In June 1964, the German authorities instigated criminal proceeding against Peiper in relation to the Boves massacre in Italy in 1943. The investigation continued for some four years before the German District Court closed the investigation against Peiper due to a lack of direct evidence against him in the giving of an order to his men to set fire to houses and murder innocent civilians, although it did find that men of his unit had set fire to homes and murdered innocent civilians in the village.

I believe it was the changes taking place within West Germany at that time, especially the government's apparent willingness to bring charges against former members of the nation's wartime forces, which left Peiper somewhat subdued and ultimately led to him leaving Germany for France. Maybe he felt he should have been treated better, like a hero rather than the war criminal he was.

Chapter Fourteen

Peiper's Death

Friday 16 July 1976 saw an article appear in that day's edition of the *Aberdeen Press and Journal.*

> Paris. A gang of anti-Nazi avengers yesterday claimed responsibility for killing convicted Nazi war criminal Joachim Peiper, and said they would strike at former SS leaders in West Germany.
>
> 'The Avengers' phoned a Paris newspaper to say they killed Peiper (61), a former SS Colonel convicted of ordering the execution of 71 American PoWs in Belgium during the Ardennes counter offensive in 1944.
>
> Peiper's home in Eastern France was burned down early Wednesday and Police said they were almost certain a charred bullet-ridden body found inside was that of the ex-Nazi, a one time member of SS Chief Heinrich Himmler's general staff.

The obvious question is, if the body recovered from the burnt out building in the French village of Traves, was so badly burnt that it was unidentifiable, was it actually Peiper's, or was it somebody else's left there to make the authorities believe it was. Although all the indications point to it being Peiper's remains, there still remains that miniscule element of doubt.

In the aftermath of the killing of Joachim Peiper on 13 July 1976, a small article appeared in the *Daily Mirror* newspaper dated Friday 30 July 1976, under the heading 'Nazi terror hits village'.

> Panic swept a village after a Nazi threat to avenge the murder of a former SS officer who lived there.
>
> An anonymous telephone caller with a German accent said the isolated village of Traves in eastern France, would be burned.
>
> Ten of the villagers would also die in reprisal for the death of Colonel Joachim Peiper, said the caller.
>
> Heavily armed police were sent to the village.

It was never discovered who made the phone call, and no such reprisal was ever carried out.

The *Daily Mirror* dated Tuesday 3 August 1976 included an article on page 9 concerning Peiper's death.

> **Curious Case of the SS Colonel**
> There is a curious English connection in the bizarre killing of Joachim Peiper, the SS Colonel apparently killed by a French Resistance execution squad at his home in a remote French village.
>
> Police investigating the assassination believe that a telephone conversation about a book by a Sandhurst lecturer, Dr Christopher Duffy, may have signed his death warrant.
>
> Peiper, police investigators now believe, was overheard by his enemies discussing military tactics on the telephone. They believed he was plotting some Nazi revival, and decided to kill him.
>
> In fact Peiper, who translated into German Duffy's book on the armies of Frederick the Great, was going over some fine points of the battles Frederick took part in, with the German publishers.
>
> Dr Duffy, who is a military historian in the Department of War Studies and International Affairs at Sandhurst, tells me that Peiper, who served ten years for his part in the massacre of American prisoners-of-war in Belgium in 1944, did translate his book.
>
> 'Although he had a ghastly past, he did a first class job of translation', he said.

Of all the people Dr Duffy could have chosen to translate his book, he chose an ex-SS colonel, and a convicted war criminal. It beggars belief that someone would actually do that, especially somebody who was helping to shape and educate Britain's future Army officers at the Royal Military Academy at Sandhurst.

An interesting point to note is that Peiper worked for the German publisher Stuttgarter Motor-Buch Verlag, but under the pen name of Rainer Buschmann. How Dr Duffy knew his true identity is unclear. The book in question is *Frederick the Great: A Military Life*, and was eventually published in 1985.

The village where Peiper lived was Traves, in the region of Haute-Saone. He had moved there with his wife in around 1971, and they built a home on the outskirts of the village, which they named Le Renfort, on a piece of land they had purchased by the Soane River. It was nothing too extravagant, just an average-sized three-bedroom house that was set well back from the road which provided a certain amount of seclusion. It had a veranda stretched out across the back of it, which meant that the Peipers could enjoy many a spring and summer afternoon and early evening sat out in it.

Traves was a small village with less than 300 inhabitants, but it was still a strange choice of place to live for a man who had been a colonel in the SS. Although Peiper wasn't personally implicated in any massacres within France, there had been a number of such events which had been perpetrated by German forces throughout the war. This included units of the SS.

One notable event was the Tulle massacre which took place on 9 June 1944, just three days after the D-Day landings at Normandy, that was carried out by troops of the 2nd SS Panzer Division Das Reich. They had routed members of the Maquis, French Resistance fighters, from Tulle before arresting all men in the town aged between 16 and 60. Of these, ninety-nine were hanged. But the deaths didn't end there. A further 149 of the town's men were sent to Dachau, where 101 of them died.

On 10 June 1944, the same SS unit carried out another massacre in the village of Oradour-sur-Glane, where 642 of the village's residents, including women and children, were murdered. The village was rebuilt after the war, but on land nearby. Charles de Gaulle, the wartime president of France, decided that the remnants of the original village should remain as a permanent memorial to those who had been so savagely murdered by the Germans.

Peiper spent his time in Traves working as a translator. Much of his work related to the translation of military related books from English to German. The French authorities not only knew Peiper was living in Traves, but on 27 April 1972 they had granted him a residence permit valid for five years. Strangely enough, Peiper wasn't the only ex-member of the SS living in the village at the time. Erwin Ketelhut, who had been a captain in the Leibstandarte artillery, was Peiper's nearest neighbour, living just 250 yards away.

Peiper and his wife, Sigurd, led a relatively quiet life in the village, but for whatever reason they had decided not to change their names, despite the fact that as a translator, Peiper used the name Rainer Buschmann.

All was well for Peiper and Sigurd until 1974 when a former unnamed member of the French Resistance, who was either a member of the Communist Party or who had communist sympathies, revealed Peiper's grizzly past and true identity to the French Communist Party. Surprisingly, nothing of any real significance happened immediately. It would be another two years before matters came to a head. On 21 June 1976, notices began appearing all over Traves outlining

Peiper's wartime service with the SS, and his connection with the murder of American soldiers at Malmedy along with Belgian civilians in surrounding villages, as well as the murder of twenty-three civilians in Boves, Italy.

A French daily newspaper, *L'Humanite*, which at the time was believed to have had connections with the French Communist Party, included an article about Peiper in its edition of 22 June 1976, stating where he lived and calling for him to be expelled from France. This led to graffiti appearing on walls and road surfaces throughout the village, with swastikas and Peiper's name.

In the following days and weeks a number of reporters, some from abroad, arrived in Traves, seeking an interview with the village's most notorious inhabitant, which Peiper willingly gave, explaining his side of the story and painting himself out to be the victim. He denied having been a member of the Nazi Party, claiming instead to have only been a 'soldier', and seemed genuinely surprised that his wartime service, which had been more than thirty years earlier, was being dragged up and spoken about.

Once knowledge of his wartime background as an SS officer was made public, he started to receive numerous threats both by letter and phone call, which he took extremely seriously.

Requests for official assistance fell mainly on deaf ears. Local police did provide officers to guard his home, and although this provision was only during the day, it was much better than anything the West German embassy in Paris could offer. This sudden and unwanted attention had shaken and unnerved Peiper so much that he decided it was time for him and Sigurd to return to Germany. On 12 July 1976, with his wife's safety paramount in his thoughts, he sent her back to Germany ahead of him.

The following day Peiper met up with his neighbour and ex-SS comrade Ketelhut to discuss his situation, at which time Peiper appeared to be quite calm. He wasn't convinced that anything would happen in a physical sense against him, but he had armed himself with a couple of weapons just in case it did.

Bastille Day in France is celebrated on 14 July. In the early hours of that morning Peiper's neighbour, Ketelhut, was woken by the sound of the village siren, and when he looked out of his window, he could see that Peiper's home was on fire. By the time the flames had been put out, and the police were able to get into the burnt out shell of the house, they discovered a body so badly burned that it had shrunk in size. A watch found on the body had stopped at one o'clock in the morning. They also found three firearms which, forensically, they were able to establish had all been recently fired along with the remnants of what they took to be Molotov cocktails.

An autopsy revealed that there were no bullet wounds on the badly charred remains, indicating that the individual had more than likely been overcome by smoke from the fire and subsequently died in the flames.

The following morning the strangest of events took place when Ketelhut was asked to identify the body. Whether he volunteered, or the police knew of his connection with Peiper is unclear, but Ketelhut identified the body as being that of Peiper. As the remains discovered in the house were so badly burnt, I have no idea how any such identification was actually possible. This being the case, why did the Police request Ketelhut to view the remains?

The circumstances of the events of 14 July 1976 led some to suspect that Peiper had not actually perished in the fire at all, and whomsoever's the body discovered in the burnt-out remains of the house, it wasn't his. Which version of that story is correct I have no idea, but to pretend you were dead would be a great way to get people to stop looking for you and to be able to start a new life in somewhere like Argentina perhaps.

Sigurd had the remains of her husband returned to Germany where he was buried in the cemetery at St Anna's church, Schondorf am Ammersee, Bavaria.

Nobody was ever arrested, charged or convicted of Peiper's death, although it was strongly believed that those responsible were known as the 'Avengers', a group of unidentified individuals who were believed to have either been Communists or former members of the French Resistance.

In the minds of many, particularly Americans and especially veterans of the Battle of the Bulge, Peiper's death was seen as nothing more than poetic justice, as many, if not all of them, believed he had cheated the hangman's noose thirty years earlier in 1946.

Chapter Fifteen

US Senate Committee Hearing on Armed Services, 1949

The following is taken from the minutes of a meeting of the United States Senate Committee Hearing on Armed Services, before the First Session of the 81st Congress, into the Malmedy massacre of unarmed American soldiers who had been captured and taken as prisoners of war.

The hearing was spread out over twenty-three separate days, between 18 April and 6 June 1949, the written report of which consisted of 1,670 pages. This included the evidence of thirty-three witnesses, who in some way, shape or form were involved in the investigation.

Two of those present were Senator Raymond E. Baldwin, the Senator for Connecticut, and Kenneth C. Royall, Secretary of the United States Army.

The interesting point here is that the investigation concerned the actions of those members of the United States Army with respect to their involvement with the defendants who were responsible for the massacre.

I have picked out just a few examples from the report in relation to what happened at Malmedy and how those members of the SS, including Peiper, who were arrested in relation to the massacre were dealt with by the American authorities, both at the time of their original trials and when their death sentences were subsequently commuted to terms of imprisonment.

The report, as might be expected, contains a great deal of first-hand evidence and extremely interesting discussion.

Page 6 of the report includes the following observations from Secretary Royall.

> The Malmedy cases present sharply conflicting considerations, in view of the allegations that have been made. The situation is the type which always presents difficulty to any court, or to any executive authority which must act on the life or death of persons charged with crime. It is one of the most unwelcome responsibilities that my office has, to pass on death sentences.
>
> There are rarely any in which there is not a sharp contention made. I do not know anybody charged with a crime in which the

> death penalty can be inflicted, who doesn't make sharp contentions of innocence or misconduct on the part of the court, or something. On the other hand, there is the undisputed fact that in these cases, approximately 80 American soldiers, as well as a number of innocent civilians, were slaughtered in cold blood, in total violation of all accepted rules of civilised warfare. There is nothing in the record to indicate any controversy about that fact.
>
> Most of those killed were young men called into the service of their country, young men who had proven their courage and fitness, who had served honourably and faithfully and bravely, and who were entitled to expect that if they fell in to the hands of an enemy, they would be properly treated as prisoners of war.
>
> It is one of the most atrocious crimes that I know of in all of the war crime annals. It is a crime that ought to be punished by death, if the right person can be apprehended and properly convicted and no guilty persons should escape just punishment, either through technicalities or legal refinements or overdrawn theories.

I was intrigued to note that during Secretary Royall's speech, he was not once interrupted, possibly because what he was saying was such a delicate matter, and to have interrupted could have been deemed as disrespectful to the memory of those murdered American soldiers.

> On the other hand, the contention is made that the convictions were obtained by involuntary confessions extorted by promises of immunity and by threats and force, in disregard of established rules of American justice. That is the contention of the defendants and their counsel but as to this feature of the case, those American officers and enlisted men and civilians who were charged with the preparation of these trials deny that there was any improper conduct in obtaining these confessions. If their statements are correct, then the procedures followed were proper, the confessions were voluntary, and those who were convicted have been proven guilty and should be punished.
>
> These conflicting considerations, it seems to me, must be continually borne in mind, whatever aspects of the Malmedy cases are to be studied.

The SS defendants that were referred to by Secretary Royall, included Joachim Peiper.

Senator McCarthy responded:

> I think every member of the committee has lost either a son or someone very close to him in the service. Every member of the committee realizes the gruesomeness of the crime perpetrated over there. I think every member of committee feels that when the guilty are found and properly tried, they should be either hanged or whatever sentence happens to be meted out to them. There is no desire on the part, I believe, of any Member of the Congress to see anyone who is guilty go free.
>
> However, in view of the exceptionally good record over in the Pacific where every war criminal was tried honestly and fairly, and executed as quickly as they were over in Europe, in all the unusual reports coming out of the European theatre, some of us were very much concerned in checking to see exactly what type of justice we are meting out in Germany, especially in view of the report of the Clay Committee.
>
> As I recall, General Clay appointed the judge advocate general, plus some of the members of the prosecution, to make an investigation over in the European theatre and find out how confessions or convictions were obtained, so that the extent to which we are concerned in going in to this, you might say we start with a report that Clay's own men make which they say there were mock trials, we did use physical force, that in some instances we took ration cards away from families of prisoners and in view of that we feel that we should go in to the whole matter to find out whether or not the men who were prosecuting in that area were competent to know what is meant by 'American justice'.

I was interested to note that the Americans were so intent on making sure that justice was being meted out as fairly and as honestly as it should have been. Although massacres and injustices such as Malmedy were horrendous and should never have taken place in modern warfare, it should not have been a case of 'we need to punish somebody for this crime, and if we can't find those responsible, we will punish someone, just because they are German and they will do'.

> As I say, that is doubly important, in view of the fact that over in the Pacific theatre, where the crimes were just as bad, and the persons

> were just as hard to apprehend, we apparently dealt out a good clean brand of justice.
>
> As to the gruesomeness, there is nothing that any of us can recall in recorded history that approaches the unwarranted type of mass slaughter that occurred at Malmedy, and we always like to see the men responsible brought to justice.

Senator McCarthy finished his comments with the following:

> To repeat, we are concerned with finding out how the convictions were obtained, how confessions were obtained, and how the prosecution staff worked. If they worked improperly, we want to know. If they did not follow the American concept of justice, then we think that those individual men should be brought up before your court martial to determine whether or not they should be left in charge of that kind of work, so that when we go into the next war, if there is a next war, we will know that the trials were properly conducted, and if these same men are in charge, we want to know that they conduct those matters properly.

It is interesting to note the lengths to which the United States Congress went, to ensure that American servicemen in charge of suspected German war criminals were acting in a correct and professional manner, regardless of how heinous their crimes had been.

I wonder if Peiper and his fellow convicted war criminals appreciated or knew just how hard the American authorities were working to ensure that they were treated fairly and honestly, which in some cases resulted in those sentenced to death having their sentences commuted to a term of imprisonment.

I do not believe that if the 'boot had been on the other foot', that German authorities would have conducted themselves in such a balanced manner. I suspect they would not necessarily have been driven by finding out the truth of who was responsible for having committed a similar crime, but more likely to have found certain individuals guilty, so that somebody paid – no matter who that was.

On page 15 of the report there was an exchange between Secretary Royall and Senator McCarthy. The conversation between the two men had begun about the correct way to deal with American military personnel who might have 'over-stepped the mark' when it came to their individual dealings with the German defendants, in particular how they had managed to get them to make confessions.

Senator Royall:

> Here the evidence clearly shows that all of the defendants were members of the SS and were under strict orders not to talk at all. If all legal means had not been used to induce these prisoners to talk about these occurrences, there would have been no chance at all to apprehend or convict any of those guilty of the massacre.
>
> There is one other consideration that is entitled to considerable weight. It is a natural tendency of every defendant who confesses to claim that his confession was procured by improper means. In early experience in the trial of criminal cases, and I am sure in the experience of many of you gentlemen, it is rare in a murder case where there is a confession, rare indeed for the defendant not to seek to repudiate his confession.
>
> It then becomes a question of veracity between the defendant and possibly his associates, on the one hand, and the law enforcement authorities on the other hand. These issues arise in many, many murder cases, and civil courts and, as we all know, in civil life.
>
> The testimony of the law enforcement officers, on the average, is more credible and therefore is usually accepted.
>
> Despite all this discussion, I am still of the opinion that if any of the confessions relating to the guilt of the six under death sentence were obtained by force or improper inducements or brutality, or any other improper means, and if there is not sufficient other cogent evidence to support the death sentences, then they should be commuted.

Secretary Royall also said that he was unclear as to what action should be taken against current or previous members of the American military who had been responsible for the mistreatment of any of the German defendants, and that he would be reticent to take the matter to a court martial stage, as all they were doing was trying to ensure those who were responsible for the atrocities carried out against American soldiers at Malmedy, were convicted, which after all was 'a very normal and natural human emotion'.

Senator McCarthy responded:

> This is rather important. It is a rather unusual statement you make. I was in the Marine Corps and as you know feelings ran high in all quarters for the duration of the war, in most combat areas during the war, and you felt that under the circumstances it was much more

important to protect the rights of the prisoners of that time, than during the normal peacetime.

The following interaction then took place between the two men:

> **Secretary Royall:** These were not prisoners of war.
>
> **Senator McCarthy**: Not prisoners of war?
>
> **Secretary Royall**: No. These defendants were not. The war was over. They were not captured. They were criminals who had been apprehended.
>
> **Senator McCarthy**: You don't know whether they are criminals or not until they are convicted.
>
> **Secretary Royall**: They were charged with these war crimes. They were not taken as prisoners of war, these defendants who were being tried.
>
> **Senator McCarthy**: You say they are charged with a crime.
>
> **Secretary Royall**: Yes.
>
> **Senator McCarthy**: And you and I will agree, I assume, that when a man is charged with an atrocious crime and when feelings run high, that is the time when we must have strict rules and regulations to protect the rights of someone who may have need of the law.
>
> **Secretary Royall**: I agree.

The conversation between the two men continued in a convivial but professional manner, with Secretary Royall having the last word as such: '….but as to the prosecution for crime, I am positive, for example, that a criminal, many war criminals tried immediately after the war were convicted who would not have been convicted 2 years later; and that is human nature'.

Page 102 of the report includes the interview of Mr Kenneth Ahrens, of Erie, Pennsylvania, who during the war had been a Sergeant with B Company of the 285th Field Artillery Observation Battalion, and was a survivor of the Malmedy massacre. When the SS soldiers opened fire on their American prisoners Ahrens was hit in the back, but instinctively knew to close his eyes, stay still and pretend that he was dead. It was a decision that saved his life. As the SS soldiers moved among the American dead and dying, they shot dead anybody who showed any sign of life. If they were not sure whether an American was alive or dead, the SS soldiers would kick them and if they heard so much as a murmur they would shoot them in the head.

Sergeant Ahrens didn't move a muscle or open his eyes for nearly two hours, knowing that if he did, and he was seen by one of the SS soldiers, he would be shot dead. The SS armoured column finally moved on, and when Ahrens and a number of other survivors felt that it was clear to get up, they did so and made their way back to the comparative safety of the American lines, where they were able to pass on to their senior officers detailed information about what had happened.

> **Senator Baldwin**: Mr Ahrens, will you stand and raise your right hand.
>
> Do you solemnly swear that the testimony you are going to give in this matter now in question, shall be the truth, the whole truth, and nothing but the truth to the best of your knowledge, information and belief, so help you God!
>
> **Mr Ahrens**: I do.
>
> [The first few questions were just to confirm his name and address, where he worked, and that during the course of the Second World War he had served in the American Armed Forces in the Army.]
>
> **Senator Baldwin**: What outfit were you with?
>
> **Mr Ahrens**: I was in the Two Hundred and Eighty-Fifth Field Artillery Observation Battalion.
>
> **Senator Baldwin**: And were you in the so called Battle of the Bulge?
>
> **Mr Ahrens**: I was.
>
> **Senator Baldwin**: And that was in December 1941?
>
> **Mr Ahrens**: That is right.
>
> **Senator Baldwin**: Can you relate to us what happened in connection with the Malmedy matter.

Before Mr Ahrens could reply, Senator McCarthy interrupted to inquire why Senator Baldwin was asking Mr Ahrens questions about the events which had happened at Malmedy, when the massacre had already been accepted by both Democratic and Republican senators as having taken place, when the committee had been set to investigate the actions of American servicemen who had dealt with those German SS officers and soldiers who were on trial for their lives. Senator McCarthy added that he felt that by bringing Mr Ahrens before the committee to give his testimony, all that Senator Baldwin was doing was attempting to put those senators who felt this thing should be investigated, into the position of appearing to defend the actions of German SS troops, which they were not.

He added that he believed it was an attempt on Senator Baldwin's part to try and inflame the public, while attempting to create the same situation in the committee which apparently existed in Germany at the time of the original trials, so as to move the topic away from looking at the actions of a number of American soldiers.

Senator Baldwin responded by saying that the only reason he had asked Mr Ahrens to speak before the Committee was to try and establish the truth of what really took place at Malmedy, and who better to hear that from than somebody who was actually there. If by listening to what Mr Ahrens said could prove or disprove what was being alleged by the German defendants and the statements they had made and signed, then surely that was a good thing.

> **Senator Baldwin:** All right sir [Mr Ahrens]. Will you describe to us where you were, and how you came upon the scene, and as briefly as you can, what happened as you observed it.
>
> **Mr Ahrens:** Well, my entire company of approximately 150 men was sent out to a town by the name of St Vith; that is in Belgium.
>
> **Senator Baldwin:** V-i-t-h?
>
> **Mr Ahrens:** That is right. We had been up north at this particular time and they pulled us out of there and we were being sent down to St Vith, and we were travelling in convoy; I would say 40 or 50 trucks and jeeps.
>
> Early in the afternoon of this particular day, we approached this crossroads above Malmedy and there was more or less a straight stretch of road as you go through the crossroads. You hit a straight stretch of road for approximately a mile or two. And at that point, when we got out on that road, was the first we knew of a breakthrough at all, because we were trapped right in the middle of it, and our vehicles and men were pinned down on the road from tank fire and

small arms fire, at which time I got out of my jeep and hit the side of the road until I kind of found out what was going on.

Senator Baldwin: When you say, 'hit the side of the road', do you mean you got down on the road?

Mr Ahrens: 'The road was more or less built up level with the ground, and I crawled out of my vehicle and went down more or less of a field outside the road, which practically all of the men did, because if we had stayed in the jeeps we would have been killed right there.

Senator Baldwin: In other words, you mean by that, while travelling along the road you were suddenly subjected to terrific gunfire of all kinds?

Mr Ahrens: That is right.

Senator Baldwin: Go ahead and describe what happened after that.

Mr Ahrens: At that time, not knowing, it was a complete surprise, not knowing what was going on, I made a break for some sort of a farmhouse across the road for reasons of shelter and so forth, and I laid there until I was captured. They kept us pinned down until we were captured.

Senator Baldwin: Do you know how many were captured?

Mr Ahrens: Well, my entire company, as I said before, was spread out along this road, and I would say all of them, pretty close to 150, were involved, plus some stray vehicles that had gone by or had come by at the same time. I mean the road is a through road, and therefore our troops used it to get back and forth on, and naturally there would be different companies who had men going through there, and this also was some way back off the front line. It was probably 5 or 6 miles in the rear of what we thought was a front line, so I would say it was a complete surprise being cut down that fast, not knowing what it was.

So as I laid alongside of this farmhouse, we could see these tanks rolling up the road, and the German troops all spread out through the fields and woods. They more or less had been waiting somebody to come through there because they were that far advanced through our lines at the time this happened.

So about the only thing we could do was give up. I mean we just could not fight against tank fire. We had nothing but small arms and they were using a lot more than that to keep us down. We had no choice but to throw our arms up and give up.

At that time I got up on the road with my hands up in the air, the same as the rest of the boys. I could see them lined out all the way down the road, the road that we came up on. And they proceeded to get us all in some sort of file and told us to walk back down the way we came, which is what we did during the course of that time. During the course of that walk back toward the crossroads where we had just passed, which was about half a mile above that, I saw numerous men who had been killed and wounded. Some of them were laying alongside the road. Some of them were being beat up. Some of them were being pulled out of the woods where they had been hiding to get away from the gunfire. And then they marched us back down the road, in more or less a column of men.

When they got us back to the crossroads, they searched us and took whatever they wanted to. I mean they went through our pockets and took watches, rings, and wallets, whatever we had on us.

Senator Baldwin: Had they taken your arms away from you at that time?

Mr Ahrens: We had already thrown our arms up. If we had not, they would have killed us at that time. We definitely had no choice of holding our arms, at that time I crawled up on to the road. I was hiding down there at the farmhouse. I was alongside of the farmhouse. I threw my gun away down there. If I had come upon the road with my gun I would have been shot right there. I take it that is what happened to the men I saw lying along the road. They still had their guns in their hands when they were caught.

So when they marched us back down to this crossroads, they, as I say, they searched us and pushed us all in to a field which was more or less an enclosed cow pasture. I believe it belonged to a farm. There seemed to be a small farm right there, a couple of buildings off to the side of the field, and the field ran parallel to the road. The fence was no more than 10 to 15 feet away from us. So we all crawled, or we were pushed down in to the field, in to more or less a group.

Ahrens was sat in a chair in front of a long table, with a jug of water available for him to take a drink whenever he needed it. Talking for such a long period of time in front of such a distinguished group of individuals, could not have been an easy task, as he relived what after all must have been a terrifying experience and far from easy to relive, albeit briefly.

> By the time I had got down there, there was practically my entire company lined up in that field, and everything was in quite a turmoil, and there was a lot of our boys who had already been hurt, I mean as in wounded by shell and gunfire, and a few of our medics were running round trying their best to help them, by tying up an arm or a leg, or something in an effort to stop the pain. And we stood there not knowing just what was going to happen. I mean, we had no idea what they were going to do with us, and I figured it was pretty close to Christmas and I was thinking about spending Christmas in some camp over in Germany. I mean that is what I had in my mind at that time, a terrible thought anyway.
>
> But we stood there for about half an hour, I would say, and at the same time they had lined up probably two or three tanks on the edge of the field, up on the road, and there was probably five or six troops on each tank, and they mingled around up there on the road. They watched us, and they told us to keep our hands up in the air. Every time somebody would drop their arms down a bit we would get a gun pulled out and they would aim it a little bit and they would tell us to get our hands up in the air, and that is the way we stood there, not knowing what was going to happen.
>
> But at the same time this one tank, that had finally straightened around up there on the road alongside of the field, one of their men stood up on top of it, it was either a half track or a tank, I am not sure what now.
>
> Well he pulled out his pistol while I was facing him, like all the boys were; we were just massed in a group in there, and he waved his gun in the air a little bit and aimed down into the front of our group.
>
> **Senator Baldwin**: How far were the tanks away from the road?
>
> **Mr Ahrens**: Well, I would say 20 feet, 15 to 20 feet at the most, and he aimed down in to our group and he fired once, and I noticed one of the boys drop; and he fired again and one more of the fellows dropped standing right alongside of me; and about that time, well,

I would say all hell broke loose. They just started opening up their machine guns and they really sprayed us.

Senator Baldwin: You say the machine guns opened up.

Mr Ahrens: Yes they had guns. They mounted them right on their tanks. And at that particular time I turned round and fell flat on my face.

Well, I think I was hit in the first burst or two, because I can recall being hit in the back the first time as I lay there. Well naturally that shooting went on for quite a little while, until they thought they had killed just about all of the fellows.

I know I didn't look round. I couldn't see. I mean I didn't dare look round. Just more or less because of fear, I guess and numbness.

Senator Baldwin: You were hit by the gunfire?

Mr Ahrens: Yes. One of the first bursts hit me and then I was hit again. I was hit during the course of the afternoon as I lay there. And after that happened, I don't know how long they fired in to us like that, it was quite a little while, they sprayed that group back and forth. I could tell the way the guns would get close to me and then back and forth across the group.

Well, after that ceased, I could hear them walking down among the boys that were lying there. And naturally there was a lot of moaning and groaning, and some of the boys weren't dead yet. I mean they were still alive. They had been shot up pretty bad.

So what they done, I figured what they were doing, you would hear a stray shot here and a stray shot there, they were walking around making sure that there was nobody left. Each time they would hear somebody moan, they would shoot him; and there was one particular time when I could feel, I could almost feel, a footstep right alongside of me, where one of the boys laid across the back of me, and they shot him. But why he didn't shoot me, I don't know. He must have thought I was dead because I had been hit in the back and naturally looked like I was dead.

Ahrens was very fortunate indeed. Not only because for some reason the SS soldier decided not to shoot him, but because the bullet that finished off his colleague laying across his back, did not pass through him and hit Ahrens as well.

> That went on for a little while. I don't know how long. I mean time was like years then. I could not calculate very well. But they must have moved on, and there were troops going back and forth on that road. This was their spearhead, more or less; it must have been their spearhead in this drive. And of course they were rushing troops up as fast as they could on this road and they were heading to St Vith too. That was the same road we were using. And every once and a while a tank or a half track would roll by and turn their guns on us, just for a good time; I mean they were laughing, they were having a good time. That is the way it was all during the course of the afternoon.

I can't even begin to understand what a terrifying situation it was for Ahrens and his colleagues who were still laying wounded in that field. Not only could they not move, they had to be very careful not to be seen opening their eyes or even breathing too heavily.

Chapter Sixteen

What the Papers Said

It was interesting to read what the papers had to say about the Dachau trial of the defendants of the Malmedy massacre and the subsequent events.

The *Yorkshire Observer* dated Monday 1 January 1945, included the following article on its back page:

> **Helpless Men Raked With Fire**
> **Americans Describe Malmedy Massacre**
> Results of the preliminary investigation by the American authorities into the shooting by the Germans of some 115 American prisoners near Malmedy, at the opening of von Rundstedt's recent counter offensive, were released by S.H.A.E.F last night.
>
> The massacred men were mostly from a field artillery observation battalion and their story is told by 15 who escaped. Their battery was travelling in convoy on 17 December, and arrived at the junction of the highways of St Vith and Waimes, when a number of German tanks travelling in the opposite direction were observed. The Germans opened fire immediately and the Americans abandoned their vehicles to seek cover. Shortly however, the whole battery's personnel were captured and rounded up in an open field.
>
> After taking away their valuables, the German guard suddenly fired in to the defenceless group. Shortly afterwards two German tanks began spraying the Americans with machine gun fire from between 75 and 120 feet. Dead and wounded prisoners fell to the ground, as did those who were not hit.
>
> The American authorities believe that those who were not hit at first were later killed when the German gunners continued spraying them on the ground. When the tanks left the field, German infantrymen on top of them fired small arms in to the helpless mass. Finally German soldiers walked through the mass of bodies deliberately shooting men still showing signs of life.

Between 20 and 25 Americans, who even after this were only wounded, decided to make a run for it. The German guards opened up at them again, but 15 managed to escape.

On Monday 20 August 1945, an article concerning Joachim Peiper appeared on the front page of the *Birmingham Daily Gazette*:

US Troops Find Their Man
No. 1 War Criminal was in a PoW Cage
An eight month search for the man responsible for the mass slaughter of more than 100 American infantrymen prisoners near Malmedy during the Battle of the Bulge, last December, has ended.

The criminal Colonel Joachim Peiper, aged 30, a former adjutant to Himmler, was found hiding among 10,000 SS troops in a prison camp.

His connection with the Malmedy massacre was revealed after hours of questioning. Major Clisson, commandant of the SS prisoners of war camp, said Peiper (Pfeiffer) was the US troops public enemy No.1.

Peiper had in fact surrendered to American forces in early May 1945, and had been in their custody for three months before his true identity was discovered. But that was more to do with the sheer weight of numbers of German prisoners, than any failing on the part of the Americans.

The *Sunderland Daily Echo and Shipping Gazette*, dated 31 Thursday January 1946, included the following article on its back page.

Malmedy Massacre
A documented account of the massacre of 129 unarmed US soldiers near Malmedy during the German Ardennes Offensive in December 1944 was presented.

While M. Dubost was describing the massacre, Goering hung his head, states Chas Lynch (Reuter).

A Nazi officer indulged in target practice on the 129 Americans as a prelude to their cold-blooded murder. A statement by a German soldier described the massacre at a crossroads.

The Americans were led to a field, where the Nazis searched each man, taking watches, rings and other effects. A German armoured vehicle was then manoeuvred so that its guns were trained on the Americans.

A German officer dismounted from the vehicle, took a revolver, aimed and fired. One of the prisoners fell. The officer then aimed again and another man fell.

As the second man dropped, machine-gun fire was opened up from the vehicle on the little group of prisoners, spraying lead for two or three minutes, killing most of them and injuring the others.

Later German soldiers walked among the group, and those Americans who were still alive were finished off.

'The shame of this deed will remain upon the German Army', the German soldier's statement went on. 'We knew that these men were unarmed and had surrendered.'

The Hartlepool Northern Daily Mail dated Tuesday 21 May 1946, included the following article:

Malmedy Massacre
Nazis 'Laughed as they Shot Us'
German soldiers laughed as they attacked unarmed American prisoners of war with machine guns and revolvers in a field near Malmedy, Belgium during the Germans' Ardennes push at Christmas 1944, Virgil Lary, a former US Lieutenant told the Dachau war crimes court today.

Three German generals and 71 soldiers were before the court charged with the massacre of US prisoners of war. Lary said, 'I heard sharp commands in German and then a burst of machine-gun fire directed at our group.

I fell to the ground with my face in the mud. Men fell dead and wounded all around me. The firing lasted about three minutes. Then I heard agonised screams from a wounded man. There was a single pistol shot and the screams ceased.

I heard German laughter and later more machine-gun fire, more pistol shots and more laughter.'

Lary pointed out Georg Fleps, a Rumanian SS private as the man who fired a pistol in to a group of some hundred prisoners.

The following article appeared in the edition of the *Liverpool Echo* dated Wednesday 22 May 1946.

Took 'Pot Shots'
At
US PoW
SS Men's Part in Malmedy Massacre
Samuel Dobyns of Ohio, former ambulanceman in the US Army, told a US military court here today, that German machine gunners took pot shots at American prisoners as they lay on the ground near the Belgian village of Malmedy in December 1944.

Giving evidence in the trial of 74 German SS men, including three Generals, accused of massacring US prisoners at the beginning of the Ardennes Offensive, Dobyns said he himself was wounded four times in the shooting. 'One man lying near me called out that his legs were paralysed and he asked for medical help. A German shot him in the back of the head.'

Ex-Sergeant Kenneth Frederick Ahrens said that while lying with his face in the mud he heard German soldiers laughing and 'having a helluva of a good time while our boys were praying'.

Homer Fort of Missouri said he and his comrades were taken to a field and machine gunned. Speaking of Germans taking 'pot shots', Fort said, 'I could hear the bullets thudding in to the bodies of my groaning comrades.'

You have to wonder how different things would have been if none of the American soldiers had survived the massacre. There would have been no such first-hand accounts as told by Ahrens, Dobyns and Fort. The families of the murdered men would never have found out what had actually happened to their loved ones, and the true circumstances of their deaths. All they would have been told was that their son, brother or husband had been killed in action while serving their country.

Saturday 8 June 1946 saw an article appear in the *Belfast News-Letter*:

Dagger in Back
A German witness's Fear
Dachau, Friday. Sergeant Otto Wichmann, a German, told a United States court here today that he was afraid he would one day get a dagger in his back for giving evidence.

He had been called in the trial of 74 German SS men accused of murdering US troops at Malmedy Belgium.

> In a written statement, Wichmann said he feared that he would be stabbed when he was free again, 'because in conformity with truth, I told that SS Colonel Peiper ordered me to shoot frozen, exhausted United States prisoners of war'.

This raises an interesting point because although Wichmann was most definitely at the Dachau war crimes trial in May 1946 to give evidence against Joachim Peiper, it wasn't in relation to any events which had taken place at Malmedy in December 1944. Wichmann's evidence against Peiper was for an event which took place at the Petit Their Chateau, which at the time was a German Panzer Tank Regiment Command Post. He could not be certain as to the actual date of the event, but believed it took place sometime between late December 1944 and early January 1945.

An American soldier who had been hiding out in a nearby, snow-laden forest, was cold, hungry, exhausted and could take no more, so he decided to surrender and hand himself in to the first German soldiers he came across.

The unnamed American prisoner was handed over to SS-Unterscharfuhrer Otto Wichmann, who in turn took him to the Panzer Regiment command post where Peiper, Hans Gruhle, Poetschke and Dr Sickel were sitting round a wood stove. Peiper briefly interrogates the man, who he can see is clearly exhausted, suffering from exposure and frostbite. Dr Sickel orders Wichmann to kill the prisoner, which he does by shooting him.

The *Gloucestershire Echo* dated Wednesday 19 May 1948 carried the following article on its front page.

> **Execution of 17 Germans**
> **Stayed**
> The US Army Secretary, Mr Kenneth Royall, last night stayed the executions of 17 Germans sentenced to death for a wartime massacre of unarmed American prisoners, after the Supreme Court had refused to consider an application for release, says a Washington message today.
>
> He said that 'serious allegations' in the petition would be investigated by the US Military Commander General Clay.
>
> The 17 Germans were convicted at Dachau of complicity in the 'Malmedy massacre'.
>
> The mass appeal to the Supreme Court, carrying 74 names of German prisoners convicted of war crimes, was filed by Mr Willis M. Everett, American ex-Army officer who defended them.

He alleged that the United States had used 'sham' courts, threats, and third degree methods in forcing confessions from the prisoners.

The Government filed no answer.

It was an interesting turn of events. The American lawyer who had defended the seventy-four men, including Joachim Peiper, at their original Dachau trial, men tried for the murder of unarmed American prisoners of war, had taken their case to the highest court in America, with the result that the US Army Secretary had prevented the executions from going ahead.

At the time of the trial, Everett, an American lawyer from Atlanta, Georgia, had been a colonel in the United States Army. He was convinced that none of the German defendants had received a fair trial. To support his claims he highlighted the fact that the men were made to endure the stress of undergoing mock trials which were carried out by those involved in their interrogation as a means of getting them to talk. In addition, they had all been kept in solitary confinement in the dark, and had their food rations greatly reduced. On top of this, Everett further claimed that the men had been subjected to physical torture which included the sustaining of broken bones and for some, injury to their testicles.

The intervention by Kenneth Royall led to the Simpson Investigation, looking into not only the Malmedy massacre case, but other cases that had also been dealt with by American International Military Tribunals throughout Europe, in the immediate aftermath of the war.

The *Bradford Observer*, dated Tuesday 6 September 1949, included the following article:

Mock trials caused Nazi SS troopers to confess

Four Americans who helped to convict 73 SS troopers of the Malmedy massacre admitted yesterday that they had used mock trials and tried to 'scare' confessions out of suspects. But they denied brutality.

They were testifying before a three man sub-committee of the United States Senate which is investigating the German convicts' charges of maltreatment. The lives of six men may hinge on the outcome.

The six are still under death sentence for their roles in the slaughter of some 700 American prisoners of war near Malmedy, Belgium, during the Battle of the Bulge.

Bruno Jacob (New Jersey), an interpreter, was the only one of the four Americans who admitted he had even heard of any maltreatment.

Jacob also admitted that suspects who refused to make confessions were sometimes put in a so-called death cell to scare confessions out of them.

All admitted the use of mock trials with fake judges presiding over benches decorated with candles and crucifix.

Harry Thon (New York), a former war crimes interpreter said the mock trials were not very effective in producing confessions. He said it took four weeks of questioning before any of the 600 suspects would admit any shooting of unarmed prisoners.

In the mock trials, the witnesses related, one investigator would play the role of prosecutor and another would pretend to be counsel for the defence. The defences counsel was supposed to gain the suspects' confidence and get them to talk.

They denied that they pronounced death sentences on people who refused to confess and that they pretended to be starting the executions.

On Wednesday 31 January 1951, the *Belfast Telegraph* carried the following article:

21 Nazis Escape Gallows Reprieved after reviews of death sentences. Seven are told they must Hang

Twenty-one German war criminals were spared from the gallows today, including six SS troopers convicted of murdering US soldiers in the infamous 'Malmedy massacre' in which 142 unarmed US prisoners were machine gunned in 1944.

Their death sentences were commuted to prison terms by the US High Commissioner, Mr John McCloy, and the US Military Commander, General Handy.

The men written about in this article were not just involved solely in the Malmedy massacre case, but in other atrocities as well. But it was the Malmedy trial, and the treatment of the defendants who were on trial at Dachau Concentration Camp in 1946, that sparked the review in to these other cases, as it was deemed their confessions were obtained through beatings and promises. The reprieved men had been held as prisoners under threat of death since the end of their trials in 1946.

General Handy announced the commutation of the death sentences to life imprisonment for the six SS troopers involved in the Malmedy massacre, but at the same time said: 'This does not mean that there is any doubt whatsoever that each defendant was guilty of the offences charged.'

As though trying hard to justify the commutations, the article went on to state:

> The offences were associated with a confused, fluid and desperate combat action, a last attempt to turn the tide of Allied successes.
>
> The crimes are definitely distinguishable from the more deliberate killings in concentration camps. Moreover, these prisoners were of comparatively lower rank and were neither shown to be the ones who initiated nor advocated the idea of creating a wave of frightfulness.
>
> Mr McCoy said, 'I am satisfied that the dispositions now finally made are just to the individual and to society. I have striven to temper justice with mercy.'
>
> All the SS troopers remaining under the death sentence for the Malmedy massacres were saved from the gallows by General Handy's ruling. This means that no German will be executed for one of the worst atrocities of the war.
>
> Several hundred captured, unarmed US soldiers were shot down in cold blood by SS troops in and near Malmedy, Belgium, during the Battle of the Bulge.
>
> Seventy-four SS men were tried by a US Military Court in 1946 on charges of participating in these shootings. Seventy-three were convicted and 43 were sentenced to hang, but subsequent reviews brought commutations of the death sentences to all but six. These were the six cases ruled on today by General Handy.

What really caught my attention is the assertion that, 'The offences were associated with "a confused, fluid and desperate combat action",' and that 'The crimes are … distinguishable from the more deliberate killings in concentration camps.'

I would respectfully have to disagree with this. What took place at Malmedy on 17 December 1944, was premeditated, cold-blooded murder. There was nothing confused about it at all, and to suggest there was is being disrespectful to the memories of those men who were murdered.

The assertion was made in an attempt to justify the possibly politically motivated decision to stay the remaining six death sentences imposed on some of those responsible.

The *Birmingham Daily Gazette* and the *Birmingham Daily Post* newspapers, of Monday 24 December 1956, both carried the following article about Joachim Peiper.

> **SS Colonel Released**
> Former SS Colonel, Joachim Peiper, condemned to death ten years ago for his role in the Malmedy massacre of 142 American PoWs was reported to be in seclusion at his family home near Baden-Baden yesterday after his release from Landsberg war crimes prison.
>
> Peiper's death sentence was commuted to life imprisonment in 1951 and later reduced to 35 years. The decision to parole him was made by a mixed German-Allied review board which does not make public its findings.

One of those who had originally fought Peiper's corner and tried to secure his release from prison was General Heinz Wilhelm Guderian. He was one of those responsible for the design and implementation of the Panzer Division, and at the beginning of the Second World War, he led an armoured corps into Poland. At the time of the Ardennes Offensive he commanded Germany's armoured units which overwhelmed the Allied defences at the Battle of Sedan.

Guderian surrendered to American forces on 10 May 1945, and despite being responsible for the troops who carried out the Commissar Order during Operation Barbarossa in 1941, and having been implicated in the German reprisals after the Warsaw Uprising of 1944, he was released in 1948 without being charged with a single offence in any war crime trial.

In 1950, his autobiography, *Panzer Leader* was published, which went on to become a bestseller, although it conveniently did not include any mention of his close relationship with Adolf Hitler, the Nazi Party, or any war crimes in which he may have been implicated. He is also believed to have cooperated with the Allies, by providing them with some 'useful' information about some of his ex-colleagues. If true, that could possibly be the reason why he was never charged with any war crimes.

In a letter to a former comrade in 1951, he wrote: 'At the moment I'm negotiating with General Handy because he wants to hang the unfortunate Peiper. McCloy is powerless, because the Malmedy trial is being handled by Eucom, and is not subordinate to McCloy.

Guderian died on 14 May 1954 at the age of 65.

As for Peiper, he was the last of those who were convicted of the Malmedy massacre to be released from Landsberg Prison. A condition of his release was the ability to show that he could find himself a job, which it must be said could not have been the easiest of things to do in a post-war Germany still struggling to deal with the shame heaped upon the nation by the actions of those who were members of the Nazi Party, the SS and the Gestapo.

Unfortunately for the rest of mankind, but fortunately for men such as Peiper, the SS were alive and kicking. Albert Prinzing, a German economist during the reign of the Nazi Party, of which he had been a member since 1934, also held the rank of Hauptsturmführer in the SS. Prinzing too had been held in detention by the Americans after the end of the war and was released in 1948.

It was with the help of Prinzing that Peiper managed to find employment in the technical division of Porsche in Stuttgart, although as we have seen, his past caught up with him and his employment there did not last long.

The influence of the SS was still prevalent in Germany fifteen years after the end of the war. In June 1960 an SS reunion took place in Windshelm and some 1,500 SS veterans met up for a few beers and a chat about their wartime experiences. One person who most definitely was not invited to the SS get-together was Sepp Dietrich. In fact it was made abundantly clear to him that he was not welcome to the two day event.

Epilogue

Joachim Peiper is somewhat of an enigma. If it hadn't been for the massacre at Malmedy, he would quite possibly have been nothing more than a minor footnote of history.

He was a colonel in the SS and well thought of by his peers as being an effective and dynamic soldier; a man respected by those who served under his command. As we have seen, Peiper was a recipient of the Knight's Cross for his actions in the Third Battle of Kharkov in February 1943. Just two months later, on 6 May 1943, he was further awarded the Deutsches Kreuz in Gold, (the German Cross in Gold). He was once again in command of the 3rd Battalion, of the 2nd Panzergrenadier Regiment LSSAH.

The citation for this award, was as follows:

> Peiper was ordered to take Zmiev and make contact with the 320 Infanterie Division. Peiper carried out this mission and brought back 750 wounded from the 320 Infanterie Division. While doing so he completely destroyed an enemy snowshoe battalion, which blocked his way back.

These actions most definitely raised his profile and at just 28 years of age, Peiper was the perfect image of bravery needed by the Nazi propaganda machine to provide the German people with a real life 'superhero' to raise their morale during the difficult months ahead. If only the German people knew how long they actually had before their leaders would capitulate.

His reputation was heightened greatly by glowing reports of his acts of derring-do in German newspapers, which in some people's eyes gave him the status of a cult figure. The Waffen-SS newspaper, *Das Schwarze Korps* (The Black Corps) was published free of charge every Wednesday and by 1944 had a circulation of around 750,000 readers. In April 1943, it ran an article specifically about the exploits of Joachim Peiper:

> In preparation for the attack on Kharkov, on his own initiative SS-Sturmbannführer Peiper twice seized bridgeheads which

> proved of decisive importance in the advance of attacking forces. Nevertheless, SS-Sturmbannführer Peiper was the master of the situation in all its phases. Every officer and man of Kampfgruppe Peiper had the feeling of absolute safety. Here a man was thinking and caring for them, made his decisions quickly, and issued his orders with precision. These decisions and orders were often bold and unorthodox, but they were issued from a sovereign command of the situation. Everyone sensed the intellectual work and the instinctive safety behind this. Of course, the commander also had soldier's luck. The unconditional trust of his men, however, has its basis in something else, namely the feeling that a born leader was in command, one filled with the highest sense of responsibility for the life of every single one of his men, but who is also able to be hard if necessary. But always the orders and measures stem, not from clever deliberation, but rather from a personality whose heart, brain, and hands are the same.

In Peiper, the German propaganda machine had discovered a gold mine. He was everything they could possibly have wanted to keep the morale of the civilian population high in difficult times. Peiper was young, good looking, enigmatic, and an excellent officer and soldier; as more of his exploits were written about, the more the German people took him to their hearts. Maybe it was also one of the reasons why he was personally awarded so many medals for the collective work of his men, because the Nazi propaganda machine needed to keep his profile as high as they possibly could. What better way than award him military medals. It simply made him more marketable to the German public.

After the war, with the Americans knowing Peiper's connection to the Malmedy massacre and believing him to be alive, what better person to put before a military tribunal, convict of war crimes and make sure he is sentenced to death. If the Americans killed Peiper in this way they would achieve two things: they would reduce a national hero to a common criminal, while at the same time punish him for the murders of the American soldiers.

Regardless of the magnitude of that offence, what became apparent was the lack of physical evidence against Peiper. For a start, I have not discovered, seen, or heard of anybody who was able to confirm Peiper was present at Malmedy, at the time when the massacres took place.

If Peiper was tried today in an unbiased civilian court for the same offence as he was at Dachau in the American military tribunal in 1946, it is possible he would be found not guilty. There most certainly wasn't any forensic or documentary evidence which linked him to the Malmedy massacre. He was convicted purely on the evidence provided by a small number of his own men, who maybe saw it as an opportunity to preserve their own lives by blaming him for their individual actions.

At his trial there were a total of seventy-four defendants. Statements and admissions had been obtained from some of these men against him by what can only be described as questionable methods. If such little evidence was available, how was it possible to convict a man of war crimes and determine that the punishment to fit the crime was death by hanging?

There were other aspects of the trial which I found intriguing. First, the choice of location. Why Dachau concentration camp in Germany? Why not a village hall in Malmedy, Belgium, near to where the massacre of the American soldiers took place? Dachau was synonymous with death, murder and evil. By the time of Peiper's trial in May 1946, the whole world knew of the evil which had taken place there.

This raises the question of whether Dachau was chosen as the location for the trial deliberately, to paint Peiper and his comrades in a bad light even before their trial had started. Was it an attempt by American authorities to provide a subliminal backdrop of evil in the hope that public perception of the men would be cast in a similar light?

In May 2015, an article appeared in the *MailOnline*, the electronic version of the *Daily Mail* in the UK, which concerned a number of letters written by a United States Army doctor, Captain David Wilsey, sent home to his wife Emily in America, and later discovered by their daughter. The content of the letters included how, after Dachau concentration camp had been liberated in May 1945, he had seen American soldiers shoot 'SS beasts' after having lined them up against a wall. In some cases Wilsey claims, the SS guards were tortured before they were shot dead. He described how he saw one American Combat Engineer shoot dead three Nazis, to avenge a brother's death. He explained how he had calmly watched SS guards 'massacred' by US soldiers, because they 'so had it coming'.

One of his letters included how, on having witnessed the massacre of the SS guards, he had not felt a 'single disturbed emotion', because he saw the Nazis as 'SS Beasts' who deserved to be slaughtered.

The number of SS guards who were murdered by the American soldiers varies from anywhere between 30 to 500, but regardless of how many of them were murdered, not one US soldier was put on trial.

The comparison between the massacre of SS guards by American troops at Dachau and Chenogne, and the one carried out by German forces at Malmedy, is difficult to ignore. One group were prosecuted while the others were not. A classic case of, 'to the victors comes the spoils', if ever there was one.

I have no doubt that atrocities were carried out by both sides during those last months of the war, and that the only thing which separates those actions, is that in war those who are victorious are the ones that go on to determine what was right and wrong, acceptable and unacceptable, and ultimately, who will be charged with war crimes.

If Nazi Germany had won the war, British Prime Minister Winston Churchill, President of the United States Harry S. Truman, and individuals such as Marshal of the RAF Sir Arthur Harris, the wartime chief of Bomber Command, would undoubtedly have been put on trial for war crimes.

Appendix

List of the names of the eighty-one American soldiers who were murdered by German SS units during the Malmedy massacre of 17 December 1944.

Private Donald Bloom.
Technician 5th Class Carl H. Blough.
Technician 5th Class Charles R. Breon.
Corporal Joseph A. Brozowski.
Technician 5th Class Samuel P. Burkett.
Private 1st Class L.M. Burney.
Private Paul R. Carr.
Private 1st Class Homer S. Carson.
Private 1st Class Frederick Clark.
Private 1st Class John J. Clymire.
Private James H. Coates.
Private John H. Cobbler.
Private First Class Robert Cohen.
Technician 5th Class John D. Collier.
Technical Sergeant Paul G. Davidson.
Private 1st Class Warren Davis.
Private 1st Class Howard C. Desch.
Private William J. Dunbar.
Corporal Carl B. Fitt.
Private 1st Class Donald P. Flack.
Sergeant Walter A. Franz.
Private 1st Carl B. Frey.
Staff Sergeant Donald E. Geisler.
1st Lieutenant Carl R. Genthner.
2nd Lieutenant Solomon S. Goffman.
Technician 5th Class Charles F. Haines.
Private 1st Class Charles E. Hall.
Private Samuel A. Hallman.
Corporal Sylvester V. Herchelroth.

Corporal Ralph J. Indelicato.
2nd Lieutenant Lloyd A. James.
Technician 5th Class Wilson M. Jones (Junior).
Corporal Oscar R. Jordan.
Sergeant Alfred Kinsman.
Private 1st Class John Klukavy.
Technician 5th Class Howard W. Laufer.
Technician 5th Class Alfred Lengyel (Junior).
Corporal Raymond E. Lester.
Technician 4th Class Selmer H. Leu.
Sergeant Benjamin Lindt.
Technician 4th Class Allen M. Lucas.
Technician 5th Class James E. Luers.
Corporal Lawrence Martin.
1st Lieutenant Thomas E. McDermott.
Technician 3rd Class James G. McGee.
Technician Sergeant William T. McGovern.
Technician 5th Class Robert L. McKinney.
Corporal Halsey J. Miller.
Captain Roger J. Mills.
Corporal William H. Moore.
Private Keston E. Mullen.
1st Lieutenant John S. Munzinger.
Private 1st Class David M. Murray.
Corporal David T. O'Grady.
Private 1st Class Thomas W. Oliver.
Staff Sergeant John D. Osborne.
Private 1st Class Paul L. Paden.
Private Walter J. Perkowski.
Private Peter R. Phillips.
Private 1st Class Stanley F. Piasecki.
Private Gilbert R. Pittman.
1st Lieutenant Perry L. Reardon.
Technician 5th Class George R. Rosenfeld.
Corporal Carl H. Rullman.
Technician 4th Class John M. Rupp (Junior).
Private Oscar Saylor.
Technician 5th Class Max Schwitzgold.
Private Wayne L. Scott.

Technician 4th Class Irwin M. Sheets.
Private John M. Shingler.
Sergeant Robert J. Snyder.
Sergeant Alphonse J. Stabulis.
Technician 4th Class George B. Steffy.
Corporal Carl M. Stevens.
Technician 5th Class Luke S. Swartz.
Private Elwood E. Thomas.
Private 1st Class Elmer W. Wald.
Private 1st Class Richard B. Walker.
Technician 5th Class Thomas F. Watt.
Technician 5th Class Vester H. Wiles.
Technician 5th Class Dayton E. Wusterbarth.

Sources

Books

Agte, Patrick, *Jochen Peiper; Kommandeur Panzerregiment Leibstandarte* (1998).

Gallagher, Richard, *Malmedy Massacre* (1964).

Longerich, Peter, *Heinrich Himmler.* (2012).

Parker, Danny S., *Hitler's War: The Life and Wars of SS Colonel Jochen Peiper* (2014).

Westemeir, Jens, *Joachim Peiper: A Biography of Himmler's SS Commander* (2007).

Websites

www.britishnewspaperarchive.co.uk
www.warfarehistorynetwork.com
www.web.archive.org
www.historyplace.com
www.gpo.gov
www.historyonline.com
www.ns-archive.de
www.military.wikia.org
www.merriam-press.org
www.eriehistory.org
www.loc.gov
www.defence.pk
www.meetingmostre.com
www.studipiemontesi.it
www.santiebeati.it
www.11tharmoreddivision.com
www.fampeople.com

Author Biography

Stephen is a happily retired police officer having served with Essex Police as a constable for thirty years between 1983 and 2013. His wife, Tanya, is also his best friend.

Both his sons, Luke and Ross, were members of the armed forces, collectively serving five tours of Afghanistan between 2008 and 2013. Both were injured on their first tour. This led to his first book: *Two Sons in a Warzone – Afghanistan: The True Story of a Father's Conflict*, which was published in October 2010.

Both of his grandfathers served in, and survived, the First World War; one with the Royal Irish Rifles and the other in the Mercantile Navy, while his father was a member of the Royal Army Ordnance Corps during and after the Second World War.

Stephen corroborated with one of his writing partners, Ken Porter, on a previous book published in August 2012, *German PoW Camp 266 – Langdon Hills*. It spent six weeks as the number one best-selling book in Waterstones, Basildon, between March and April 2013. They have also collaborated on four books in the 'Towns & Cities in the Great War' series by Pen and Sword. Stephen has independently written other titles for the same series of books, and, in February 2017, his book, *The Surrender of Singapore – Three Years of Hell 1942–45*, was published. This was followed in March 2018 by *Against All Odds: Walter Tull – The Black Lieutenant*. October 2018 saw the publication of *Animals in the Great War* in January 2019, and *A History of the Royal Hospital Chelsea – 1682–2017: The Warriors Repose*. These last two books were written with his wife, Tanya. March 2019 saw the publication of *Disaster before D-Day: Unravelling the Tragedy of Slapton Sands*. In March 2020, *Mystery of Missing Flight F-BELV* was published, which included the personal story of the death of his uncle during the Vietnam war. The same month saw the publication of Briton *City of London at War 1939-45*. April 2020 saw the publication of *Holocaust: The Nazis' Wartime Jewish Atrocities*. In June 2020, his book entitled *Churchill's Flawed Decisions: Errors in Office of the Greatest Britain*, was published, and this was followed by *The Rise & Fall of Imperial Japan* and *Countering Hitler's Spies: British Military Intelligence – 1940–1945*.

Stephen has co-written three crime thrillers which were published between 2010 and 2012 and centre round a fictional detective named Terry Danvers.

When he is not writing, Stephen and Tanya enjoy the simplicity of going out for a morning coffee, or walking their four German Shepherd dogs early each morning, while most sensible people are still fast asleep in their beds.

Index